T0271116

Performance Measurement in Non-Profit Organizations

Performance Measurement in Non-Profit Organizations: The Road to Integrated Reporting addresses the issue of performance measurement in nonprofit companies with the aim of defining a system of useful measures to understand, manage, and improve the performance of such companies by employing systems theory to examine their conditions of existence and manifestations of life. From the proposed company model follows that the system of performance measures should make it possible to keep under control both the productive transformation, with the physical-technical efficiency indicators, and the economic transformation, with the economic efficiency indicators, and the financial transformation with the financial efficiency indicators, and finally the managerial transformation with the effectiveness indicators, taking into account the degree of satisfaction of the expectations of the main categories of company stakeholders.

Readers will understand that economic analysis alone is not sufficient to assess the performance of such organizations, but it is necessary to unite it with the analysis of sustainability dimensions. It would therefore be appropriate to draw up an integrated report that combines the economic and financial dimensions with the pillars of sustainability, as in the case of companies in the second sector. There is a gap in the literature in this area that this book aims to fill, making it a valuable resource to researchers, academics, and advanced students interested in performance evaluation of NPOs.

Patrizia Gazzola is an Associate Professor in the Department of Economics at the University of Insubria (VA), Italy.

Stefano Amelio is an Assistant Professor in the Department of Economics at the University of Insubria (VA), Italy.

Routledge Focus on Business and Management

The fields of business and management have grown exponentially as areas of research and education. This growth presents challenges for readers trying to keep up with the latest important insights. *Routledge Focus on Business and Management* presents small books on big topics and how they intersect with the world of business research.

Individually, each title in the series provides coverage of a key academic topic, while collectively, the series forms a comprehensive collection across the business disciplines.

The Innovative Management Education Ecosystem
Reskilling and Upskilling the Future Workforce
Jordi Diaz, Daphne Halkias and Paul W. Thurman

Management and Labor Conflict
An Introduction to the US and Canadian History
Jason Russell

Creativity, Innovation and the Fourth Industrial Revolution
The da Vinci Strategy
Jon-Arild Johannessen

Performance Measurement in Non-Profit Organizations
The Road to Integrated Reporting
Patrizia Gazzola and Stefano Amelio

Risk Management Maturity
A Multidimensional Model
Sylwia Bąk and Piotr Jedynak

For more information about this series, please visit: www.routledge.com/ Routledge-Focus-on-Business-and-Management/book-series/FBM

Performance Measurement in Non-Profit Organizations

The Road to Integrated Reporting

Patrizia Gazzola and Stefano Amelio

Routledge
Taylor & Francis Group

NEW YORK AND LONDON

First published 2022
by Routledge
605 Third Avenue, New York, NY 10158

and by Routledge
4 Park Square, Milton Park, Abingdon, Oxon, OX14 4RN

*Routledge is an imprint of the Taylor & Francis Group, an
informa business*

Library of Congress Cataloguing-in-Publication Data
Names: Gazzola, Patrizia, author. | Amelio, Stefano, author.
Title: Performance measurement in non-profit organizations :
the road to integrated reporting / Patrizia Gazzola and Stefano
Amelio.
Description: New York, NY : Routledge, 2023. | Series:
Routledge focus on business and management | Includes
bibliographical references and index.
Identifiers: LCCN 2022031167 | ISBN 9781032395883
(hardback) | ISBN 9781032395906 (paperback) | ISBN
9781003350439 (ebook)
Subjects: LCSH: Nonprofit organizations--Management. |
Nonprofit organizations--Evaluation. |
Performance--Measurement.
Classification: LCC HD62.6 .G39 2023 | DDC 658.4/01--dc23/
eng/20220805
LC record available at https://lccn.loc.gov/2022031167

ISBN: 978-1-032-39588-3 (hbk)
ISBN: 978-1-032-39590-6 (pbk)
ISBN: 978-1-003-35043-9 (ebk)

DOI: 10.4324/9781003350439

Typeset in Times New Roman
by MPS Limited, Dehradun

Contents

Introduction

The study addresses the problem of performance measurement in nonprofit organizations with the aim of devising a system of measures useful for understanding, managing, and improving the performance of such organizations.

The chapter uses a broad definition of a nonprofit organization considering, however, the universe of only those nonprofit organizations that develop, directly or even indirectly, a productive activity, not necessarily expressible in measurable units of goods or services. In this sense, the study focuses on nonprofit organizations that can be deemed capable of developing the four traditional types of transformations that characterize any production company:

a   productive transformation;
b   economic transformation;
c   financial transformation;
d   managerial transformation.

The nonprofit organization is observed as a system of productive transformation, for the procurement of goods and services, instrumental in achieving the goals set by the economic subject.

The chapter intends to address the problem of measuring the performance of such organizations by employing systemic theory to examine their "conditions of existence and manifestations of life" (Zappa, 1927, p. 30).

Performance measurement can be considered:

1   from an internal perspective, as an indicator of the company's ability to develop autopoietic behavior, continuously reintegrating the network of internal operational and cognitive processes that characterizes it;

DOI: 10.4324/9781003350439-1

2   from an external perspective, considering instead the nonprofit organization within its manifestations of existence, as an indicator of its ability to survive in the environment in which it carries out its institutional activities.

Therefore, internal performance indicators are aimed at investigating the conditions of efficiency to bring out the conditions of endogenous teleonomy (Mella, 1992) while external performance indicators are aimed at investigating the conditions of performance effectiveness to bring out the conditions of exogenous teleonomy of such organizations. When considering internal performance indicators, emphasis is placed on the relationships that exist between negative and positive economic and financial components of management.

While in businesses, the correlation between costs and revenues is summarized in profit, and the operational logic of maximum efficiency leads to management tending toward maximum cost compression and maximum revenue expansion, and while in public companies the operational logic of management is to compress costs and to consider the positive components thereof as quotas to cover them (fees-prices), nonprofit companies present an even different logic; in them, in fact, external ends are distinguished from survival needs on the one hand and the related costs of survival, or management costs, and costs of achieving ends, or institutional costs, on the other.

These companies seek positive components necessary to certainly replenish survival costs and to allow as much expansion of institutional costs as possible. The difference between positive components and operating costs represents the share that can be allocated to the achievement of the goals.

Therefore, the identification of a performance measurement system must devise indicators that are able to signal the existence of the following conditions:

- the existence of the prerequisites for the indefinite life of the company, hence, whether management has a balanced financial and economic performance;
- whether objectives have been met, once the management costs have been covered;
- whether it is operating efficiently, and thus, whether a rational use of available resources is made to cover management costs.

From the proposed organization model, it follows that the system of performance measures should make it possible to keep under control

both the productive transformation, with the physical-technical efficiency indicators, and the economic transformation, with the cost-
effectiveness indicators, as well as the financial transformation with the
financial efficiency indicators, and finally the managerial transformation with the effectiveness indicators taking into account the degree of
satisfaction of the expectations of the main categories of stakeholders.
The chapter culminates with the presentation of a system of indicators
capable of allowing an immediate check-up to highlight the presence
and continuity of the conditions of endogenous and exogenous teleonomy by constructing conceptual schemes useful for the analysis of
cognitive needs, and the identification of the different dimensions relevant to the appreciation of performance. In addition, it is highlighted
that in order to assess the overall performance of nonprofit organizations, it is necessary to juxtapose the traditional reporting tool
(financial statement) with another report, aimed at evaluating the existence of conditions of predominantly exogenous teleonomy: the
sustainability report. In recent years, another tool has become increasingly important in the for-profit sector: the integrated report. This
document, combining quantitative, qualitative, internal and external
data and information, serves as an important element for performance
evaluation for third-sector organizations as well. In particular, it is
proven that the integrated report cannot be considered as a simple
external indicator of effectiveness, but rather as a tool that combines
the dimensions of efficiency and effectiveness. The proposed system of
indicators is peculiar to each individual organization, and therefore
specific categories of indicators having normative character will not be
presented. The proposed system emphasizes a comprehensive analysis
aimed at measuring the results of the organization's system observed in
its complexity, and an analytical type of investigation related to the
formulation of suitable parameters to represent the result of the specific actions put in place to achieve the organization's objectives.

The approach used is of the interpretive-instrumental kind
(Franceschi, 1994) in which, in relation to the purposes of measurement and the economic-business characteristics and principles, the
inductive and deductive methods are used in an integrated way in a
process of causal analysis with the aim of highlighting the nexuses that
make reality comprehensible (Franceschi, 1978). It is therefore up to
the observer to identify – depending on the objectives and his or her
knowledge and experience – the dimensions and measurement tools
deemed appropriate and consistent.

The study is divided into six chapters. The first chapter establishes
the objectives to be achieved and the object of observation: the third

sector and the nonprofit organization. Some classifications are proposed in an attempt to identify the composition of this sector in Italy. The second chapter develops the application of systems theory to the companies under investigation. The basic concepts and reference models necessary to address the measurement problem are also analyzed. The third chapter, which addresses the identification and determination of relevant dimensions, discusses the criteria for designing the system and the proposed working methodology for identifying the most appropriate metrics for the organizational context under consideration. The last part, which concludes the performance measurement system planning, includes the identification of the most appropriate indicators for this task. Chapters 4 and 5 discuss the internal and external performance indicators deemed relevant, paying particular attention to the system's ability to maintain exogenous teleonomy. In particular, Chapter 5 emphasizes the importance of preparing and presenting a sustainability report for nonprofit organizations as well, going so far as to suggest the drafting of an integrated report, as for secondary-sector companies. The last chapter highlights how performance measurement is not enough, but it must be improved through a process to identify and remove weaknesses and increase levels of efficiency and effectiveness, and how performance measures are an essential element in raising the quality of management systems.

References

Franceschi, R. F. (1978). *L'indagine metodologica in economia aziendale.* Milano: Giuffrè.

Franceschi, R. F. (1994). *Il percorso scientifico dell'economia aziendale: saggi di analisi storica e dottrinale.* Torino: Giappichelli.

Mella, P. (1992). *Economia Aziendale.* Torino: Utet.

Zappa, G. (1927). *Tendenze nuove negli studi di ragioneria: Discorso inaugurale dell'anno accademico 1926–27 nel R. Istituto superiore di scienze economiche e commerciali di Venezia.* SA Istituto editoriale scientifico.

1 The Third Sector and Nonprofit Organizations

1.1 The data collection process for measuring results

In order to represent an effective performance measure, it is necessary for both accounting data and other elements and information to be framed in a logical scheme characterized by the identification of objectives (Guatri, 1997).

The subject of performance measurement of nonprofit companies has been addressed in literature over the years (Cestari et al., 2021), although from different perspectives. Poister (2003) uses a holistic approach in measuring the performance of nonprofit organizations. Cutt and Murray (2013) analyze the performance of nonprofit organizations from the perspective of effectiveness. Poister, Aristigueta and Hall (2014) use an integrated approach in measuring the performance of nonprofit organizations. Hoque and Parker (2018) more recently addressed the performance management in nonprofit organizations. Not only at the monograph level; noteworthy are the published papers through which authors highlight ways that can be used to measure the performance of nonprofit organizations (Ghani, Said & Yusuf, 2012; Hatzfeld, 2014; Micheli & Kennerley, 2005; Medina-Borja & Triantis, 2007; Velli & Sirakoulis, 2018). In particular, as argued by Moura et al. (2019) creating a performance measurement system in nonprofit organizations has become a challenge due to the diversity of such organizations. A recent literature review (Treinta et al., 2020) highlights how nonprofit organizations, given their orientation toward social and moral values, need a more complex measurement system than for-profit companies.

In order to address the problem of performance measurement in nonprofit organizations, it is deemed useful to observe reality by means of a data collection process through which the observer obtains qualitative or quantitative "data" from which to derive the information

DOI: 10.4324/9781003350439-2

needed to understand or operate. The data collection process can be abstractly broken down into distinguishable stages and only in theory placed in sequence:

a   goal positioning;
b   object identification;
c   dimension specification;
d   size determination;
e   annotation;
f   data processing;
g   data transmission;
h   use of data to obtain information (Mella, 1993).

The data collection processes are put in place for the purpose of achieving some observational goal. The data collection goal represents the purpose, the cognitive goal, to which the entire process is aimed. A distinction must be made between the purposes imposed on the data collector and those that the data collector assigns to the process. The former represents constraints external to the process, while the specific goals set by the data collector represent the goals of the process. This process is always aimed at some "object" of observation that represents the coordinates of observation on which the survey directly or indirectly focuses in order to obtain data and information.

The object of observation may present itself differently depending on the coordinates of observation, which depend on the observer's viewpoints. It is therefore of paramount importance to specify and make explicit the "point of view" of the data detector on the one hand and the data user on the other. Each measured object must be considered as an entity characterized by a plurality of dimensions. Some of these dimensions will be relevant to later stages of the process; others may not be of interest. This step is aimed at specifying the dimensions judged to be of interest in implementing the remaining steps of the process.

Determination of dimensions is the activity by which we identify the value that the dimensions of the object may take on. Some dimensions can be determined quantitatively while others lend themselves to qualitative determinations. Determination allows for two types of results: quantity and quality. The need to keep a record of these results leads to the annotation stage. By annotation we mean the procedure by which we "take note" of the results of determinations.

Data processing consists of changing the basic data in order to assign them to a different order, order processing, or in order to apply mathematical operations, mathematical processing. Annotated and processed data always undergo transmission. A phase that consists of the spatial and temporal movement of data.

A piece of data is the result of a determination, annotated in a predetermined language, using a given medium. A piece of information is a piece of data that can be used by a subject, fulfilling the objectives.

1.2 The process objectives: Performance indicators

The data collection process applied to nonprofit organizations aims to define a system of measures useful to understand, manage, and improve their performance. Attention is paid to the vast, multifaceted, and varied world of nonprofit organizations (Airoldi, Brunetti & Coda, 2020), which includes associations, foundations, social cooperatives, viewed according to the industries in which they operate, volunteer organizations operating in the fields of social and health care, charity, art protection, environmental restoration, research and culture in general, etc.

A broad definition of a nonprofit organization is used, however, considering the universe of only those nonprofit organizations that develop, directly or even indirectly, a productive activity. Production does not necessarily have to be expressed in measurable units of goods or services. The chapter intends to address the problem of measuring the performance of such organizations by employing a systems theory (Mella, 2022, 2021a, 2021b, 2017, 2014, 2012, 2008; Mella & Gazzola, 2019; Mella & Rangone, 2019; Superti Furga, 1971) to examine their "conditions of existence and manifestations of life" (Zappa, 1927, p. 30).

The study focuses only on analyzing nonprofit organizations that can be considered capable of developing the four traditional kinds of transformations that characterize any production company (Ferrero, 1968; Molteni, 1990; Onida, 1961):

a productive transformation;
b economic transformation;
c financial transformation;
d managerial transformation.

The nonprofit organization is regarded as a system of productive transformation for obtaining goods and services, instrumental to achieving the goals set by the economic stakeholder,[1] within given constraints. The process of defining the system of "measures" hereinafter analyzes the set of parameters that provide an understanding of the organization's ability to adapt to the changing conditions of the environment and pursue its medium- to long-term objectives. The measures taken into account play a fundamental role in coordinated action by drawing attention to the phenomena they represent, thus guiding decision-making processes by stimulating behaviors consistent with their improvement (Mason & Swanson, 1988). The measurement system must be able to consider both past and future situations, as well as external events along with internal organizational activities, and must include nonmonetary indicators to accompany the accounting data.

The problem of performance measurement is addressed from two perspectives:

1   from an internal standpoint, as the ability of the company to develop autopoietic behavior by continuously reintegrating the network of internal processes that characterizes it, this aspect is aimed at bringing out the conditions of endogenous teleonomy and investigating the conditions of efficiency;
2   from an external standpoint, considering instead the nonprofit organization in its manifestations of existence and thus in terms of its ability to survive in the environment in which it carries out its institutional activities, so the external performance indications are aimed at bringing out the conditions of exogenous teleonomy of such organizations and investigating the conditions of effective performance.

A performance measurement system aims to develop indicators that are able to signal the existence of the following conditions:

• the existence of the prerequisites for the indefinite life of the company, hence, whether management has a balanced financial and economic performance;
• whether objectives have been met, once the management costs have been covered;
• whether it is operating efficiently, and thus, whether a rational use of available resources is made to cover management costs.

This research is based on the consideration that for nonprofit organizations, as for other businesses, the ability to survive and develop is also determined by the availability of information and measurements that allow for a proper and conscious evaluation process of the results achieved. In harmony with the proposed conception of the organization, the performance measurement system is expected to allow the

monitoring of the production transformation with the efficiency indicators, of a physical-technical kind, the economic transformation
with the economic indicators, the financial transformation with the
financial indicators, the managerial transformation with the effectiveness indicators taking into account the degree of satisfaction of the
expectations of the main categories of stakeholders.[2] The data collection process is aimed at presenting a system of indicators, both
quantitative and qualitative, that can enable a check-up to highlight
the presence and continuity of endogenous and exogenous teleonomy
conditions of nonprofit organizations.

1.3 Observation subject: The "nonprofits"

The allocation of resources is one of the most deeply felt issues in
economic science since, as the available resources are limited in relation to the needs that man intends to satisfy, it is necessary to find the
best ways to employ and use them. This historical period seems to be
characterized by a tendency to increase the productivity of public
administrations and private forms of organizing economic activities,
which are different from those of the company and are in any case
market-oriented. A new model of public administration emerges in
which the types of intervention characterized by economic content are
multiplying. We witness the demise of some of the ideas of the past
such as the sharp contrast between a production company, characterized by the profit motive and the private nature of the corporate
entity, and a provider company, characterized by the social purpose of
the direct satisfaction of human needs and the publicistic nature of the
corporate entity. Therefore, now that the considerable differences
between public and private companies have fallen, today's economic
and social reality is articulated and complex, new forms of organizations other than the state and businesses emerge: the "nonprofits".

"Nonprofit" is the elliptical diction of "not for profit". This term is
used to identify all those activities that:

- do not set as management goal the maximization of profit, considered as the varied and eventual remuneration of the person who
  bears the economic risk;
- but which are aimed at maximizing the level of responses to needs
  considered of general interest to the community (local, national,
  supranational);
- they constitute a corporate category in their own right, as they
  reconcile;

- the needs of the community, specific to the state;
- the economic needs, specific to all businesses;
- the human needs, specific to the individual.

In order to identify the set of nonprofit organizations, it is important to have a preliminary overview within the general framework of the objects of study of business economics. Alongside the three basic kinds of economic units (Mella, 1992), consumer, production, and mixed public companies, one can identify numerous nonprofit entities (companies, institutions, organizations) that while not having only the purpose of consumption and/or production of wealth, implement consumption and/or production as a necessary – if not instrumental – activity for the pursuit of their founding purposes. By expanding the observational universe of business economics, it is possible to include units that do not directly set as the exclusive goal of their existence in the production and/or consumption of wealth but, nevertheless, develop these economic activities. In the following paragraphs we will indicate some possible interpretations of nonprofit organizations.

1.4 Nonprofits as organizations

Individuals normally do not operate in isolation, but come together in organizations to increase the efficiency and effectiveness (Mouzas, 2006; Davis & Pett, 2002) of the activity performed. Such organizations (Cavenago, 1996) are characterized by unity of purpose, co-operation among members, interaction, coordination, and functional organic specialization. Therefore, organizations represent fundamental social, political, and economic units. Organizations can pursue a wide variety of purposes such as temporary grouping for a cultural event, formation of a large corporation, etc.

Organizations can be distinguished into:

- business organizations: they aim at developing a business, defined as the production of a product for a given market;
- nonbusiness organizations: they have goals other than the previous ones such as consumption, wealth redistribution, or consensus management.

Business organizations can be further distinguished into:

a1   profit organizations: those that carry out production activity for the purpose of making profit;

a2 nonprofit organizations: those that carry out production activity without having profit as an objective.

Nonprofit organizations (Mella, 2021c) are characterized by an operational logic of economic transformation that can be summarized by the following operational rule: [cP $\rightarrow$ min $\leftarrow$ pP], to indicate the tendency to reduce the price to the level of unit cost of production or, with an equivalent meaning, to produce the minROI. ROE is also minimized and any equity capital must be contributed without expectation of profitability. In the general notion of a company, it is possible to identify a company when one observes an organization that in carrying out its founding activity, in whatever form also develops consumption and/or the production of wealth. Nonprofit organizations belong to a complex reality characterized by the heterogeneity of the activities carried out, the multiplicity of subjects to whom the activities are directed, and the different ways of acquiring and using economic resources. Therefore, a unified interpretation of the purposes, policies, behaviors, and achievements is difficult. Nonprofit organizations can be investigated from many angles, seeking a common reference capable of linking the many aspects that these organizations manifest in a manner not unlike that of other economic actors, bearing in mind that the economic aspect takes on very different connotations, characteristics, and intensity. Nonprofit organizations, given their limited resources, cannot exist as stable organizations without sustainably creating the conditions necessary for the production of goods or services responsive in terms of quantity, quality, and timing to the social needs they tend to satisfy.

1.5 The economic order of nonprofit institutions

"Nonprofits" can be considered organizations, in the sense of an entity or an institution, meaning a collection of elements and factors, personal and material energies and resources aimed at achieving common purposes. Purposes that individuals could not accomplish alone, but which the institution as a whole is capable of achieving. Nonprofit organizations express the economic dimension of nonprofit organizations, which is manifested in the continuous search for the conditions necessary for the institution's enduring life in a situation of capital and decision-making autonomy. The definition of the conditions of existence and development of nonprofit organizations characterize the economic-business quest (Tessitore, 1996). The corporate moment is instrumental in achieving the purposes of the institution, which are neither exclusively nor predominantly economic purposes. Only institutions are able to fully highlight the human activity of individuals and different social components, aimed at the achievement of ends that are difficult to classify according to defined and immutable categories. The life of institutions is constantly evolving and is related to the development and dynamics of human activities. Legally ordained, socially accepted, and protected institutions by public authorities may become less important while new activities may arise and successfully develop into new institutions that society perhaps first ignored or tolerated and then recognized. In this way, a global operator can be identified alongside the traditional operators, namely, households, businesses, and public administration, but without being mistaken for any of them.

On an institutional level, they differ from other institutions in the following characteristics:

- they are not natural primary institutions and therefore differ from households;
- they do not have as their purpose to produce remuneration for all factors of production according to market levels and therefore differ from businesses;
- they are not public and therefore differ from the state.

They do not, however, represent a residual class of subjects to be investigated with an analogical approach; the development witnessed in recent decades in Western economies has led to the rise of a new entity, whose economic-social connotations have completely original traits.

1.6 Nonprofit institutions as a connecting area

Nonprofit institutions, or rather the economic order of nonprofit institutions, are relevant if we consider that the economic activity they carry out is closely complementary and interdependent with that carried out in other classes of institutions. If we observe the evolution of economic systems, the observation of transformations in the mutual roles of households, businesses, and the state, together with nonprofit institutions becomes relevant. Nonprofit institutions can be observed as a connecting area between households, businesses, and the state. The area of nonprofit institutions intersects that of all other institutions (Airoldi, 1996).

It's an area:

- of connection, in which economic and noneconomic activities take place and which may be considered the joint responsibility of one or more classes of institutions;
- covered by nonprofit institutions because left vacant by the other three classes of institutions;
- of development of special skills based on the principles of volunteerism, solidarity, and cooperation.

It is an expanding area since, in advancing economic and social systems, the following two phenomena occur:

- the range of goods and services for which more and more specialized skills are needed is expanding;
- shifts in roles and responsibilities in the supply and demand of goods are observed.

These trends are clearly observable if we look at some of the needs that have evolved over the years. For example, the focus on environmental issues related to a public need has emerged only a few years ago and is particularly supported by nonprofit organizations that are often counterposed to public action. As another example, one can cite patient care, which in the past was for a long time provided by families and is now partly delegated not only to public facilities, if not to companies, but also to nonprofit organizations that have specialized in the various illnesses, and are directed toward the various categories of patients. Analyzing "nonprofits" as businesses does not mean drawing inspiration from business models, but using conceptual screenings suitable for understanding and evaluating the processes of resource deployment, having economic value in the context of operational combinations, aimed at achieving certain intervention results, satisfying needs, and possibly fulfilling aspirations.

In the Italian experience, nonprofit organizations are not as rooted in society as traditional operators, nor have they achieved a uniform degree of social acceptance and capacity for a lasting existence, with the exception of a few instances. They are, however, in the process of expansion and development; some of them can benefit from experience accumulated over time, others show uncertainties due to inadequate structures or systems based only on the generosity of founders or the voluntary, sometimes occasional, contribution of participants.

1.7 The universe of nonprofit organizations

Defining the universe of nonprofit organizations does not appear easy because in the literature (Laurett & Ferreira, 2018; Lyons, 2020) and in practice very differentiated positions are identified (Powell, 1987). We go from very broad definitions that take as their defining criterion that of the prohibition of profit distribution to very narrow definitions that consider nonprofit organizations to be those that meet the following requirements: private, nonprofit nature, provision for the benefit of the entire community, and not just members, of services that the state takes or could take on as its own purpose (Bassanini & Ranci, 1990). Or furthermore, they have been defined as those organizations that are directly engaged in the provision of services that are aimed at promoting the collective welfare (Abramson, 1986).

The industry boundaries are more or less extensive depending on the definition considered. Organizations that are sometimes excluded or questioned are those with political or religious purposes: churches, political parties, trade associations and unions, cooperative societies, mutual aid societies, and cultural and sports associations. All definitions are based on the use of the same set of classification criteria; the differences are due to the different weights given to the various criteria.

The recurring criteria are as follows:

* the nature of the activity carried out or the type of product offered: activities that fall under nursing, health and education are generally recognized as typical of nonprofits, other activities such as religious, political, cultural, etc. are sometimes disputed;
* the nature of the recipients: recipients can be divided into two categories: members of the organization, specific categories of people outside the organization who are in particular situations of disadvantage or need, many scholars exclude associations formed for the benefit of the members themselves;
* the nonexistence or at least the non-allocation of positive income results: nonprofit organizations are characterized by the prohibition to allocate any return on equity, but this principle, apparently shared, is subject to different interpretations;
* the private nature: this principle is also shared however sometimes it is difficult to qualify a public or private institution as it is necessary to define the parameters according to which a "nature" is either private or public;

- the structure of positive income components: they consider the importance of income from public versus private sources or the importance of revenue versus all other income;
- the presence of volunteer work, and its incidence in relation to total work.

1.8 Some classifications

There are many known classifications of subsystems of nonprofit organizations. The most significant ones can be summarized in the following.

The International Classification of Nonprofit Organizations (ICNPO) in the international research "Toward an understanding of international nonprofit sector" (Salamon & Anheier, 1992) identifies the following categories distinguishing them by areas of action:

1 culture and recreation;
2 education and research;
3 health;
4 social welfare;
5 environmentalism;
6 promotion of local community development, tenant advocacy, and housing asset development;
7 promotion and protection of civil rights;
8 philanthropic intermediaries and volunteer protection;
9 international activities;
10 entrepreneurial, professional, and trade union organizations.

Political parties and religious organizations are excluded from this classification as they fall under the class of influence associations.

The ICNPO also identifies five characteristics of nonprofits:

- formal constitution;
- private legal nature;
- self-government;
- absence of profit allocation;
- presence of voluntary work (Salamon & Anheier, 1994).

The classification proposed by Hansman (1986) is based on two criteria:

- the relative importance of the various sources of cost coverage;
- the actors exercising governance.

Regarding the sources of cost coverage we distinguish:

- sales revenue-based organizations, where the majority of revenue is determined by prices and fees paid by service users;
- organizations based on liberality, where revenues are mostly related to voluntary contributions.

Those exercising corporate governance are broken down as follows:

- donor-governed organizations, when among the governing bodies we have major funders;
- "entrepreneurial", when among the governing bodies we have individuals separate from the funders.

By cross-referencing these criteria, it is possible to obtain four classes of nonprofit organizations.

Abramson (1986) suggests a very narrow classification in which nonprofit organizations are identified as those that provide secular services to the public.

Considering a broad definition, nonprofits are companies in which the goal of profit is not pursued, but for which it is not physiologically excluded that it will be determined, should this occur, that it will have to be used for the company's own purposes and cannot be allocated, directly or indirectly, to the stakeholders. Nonprofit organizations can be defined as privately controlled organizations that are bound not to proceed, directly or indirectly, to the allocation of any positive income result achieved to the capital shareholders and, more generally, to those who exercise control over the company itself. Any positive income result, in fact, must be entirely allocated to the pursuit of statutory purposes (Hansman, 1986).

Non-income-oriented status is a characteristic that manifests itself in two ways (Anthony & Young, 1988):

- absence of residual remuneration of entrepreneurial contribution and capital invested by founding and promoting members or other capital invested by way of risk;
- limited signal significance that income takes on for the purpose of management appreciation, in terms of both effectiveness and efficiency, with regard to the purposes pursued by these institutions.

They represent organizations in which an activity is carried out whose motivations can be identified in the search for solutions to needs that are not met by businesses due to the application of the criterion of immediate financial convenience: a guiding criterion for businesses.

Nonprofit status does not rule out the realization of financial efficiency, but it highlights the intention to promote an activity not to maximize the economic value of possessed assets, but that of increasing and maximizing the level of response to needs considered worthy of disinterested attention. The characteristic of nonprofit relates to the finalistic sphere, while the instrumental activity, which enables the best pursuit of these ends by efficiently employing limited resources in relation to needs, must be carried out on the basis of the principles and criteria of business economics.

North American accounting principles identify the following main characteristics of the nonprofit corporation:

a   the acceptance of resources from lenders who do not expect to receive reimbursement or benefits proportional to the resources given;
b   the pursuit of activities that are essentially different from those of providing goods for a profit or equivalent result;
c   the absence of proprietary interests that can be sold, transferred, or redeemed or that result in the right to a distribution of any funds left over from the liquidation of the organization.

Another important business administration (Capaldo, 1996) classification divides nonprofit organizations into:

• organizations that devote production to predetermined subjects;
• organizations that devote their production for the benefit of given people or, generically, the entire community;
• organizations that devote their production to the market, or to particular categories of customers, and thus to trade.

In general, we could define nonprofit organizations as formal private organizations, managed under statute for the benefit of particular categories of individuals and characterized by the inability of those exercising decision-making power to take ownership of the value of the business. The ban concerns the distribution of profits and does not affect the production of a managerial residue.

1.9 Nonprofit organizations in Italy

The need to contain public debt and the need to improve the quality of services provided have enabled the development of nonprofit organizations, which are seen as a way to achieve both goals in the area of welfare services (especially: health, care, and education) as well as in the whole range of collective services and public utilities (such as culture, environment, territorial, and public machine arrangement) (Civitillo, Ricci & Simonetti, 2019; Terzo, Notarstefano & Di Maggio, 2022).

We shifted from the belief that the pursuit of public purposes was the exclusive task of the state to the belief that leaving more room for nonprofit organizations in the area of collective services will improve service for citizens with a lower public expenditure.

Nonprofit organizations operate in much broader areas than the traditional areas of welfare. In fact, they are present in the area of culture, entertainment, recreation seen as a time for socialization, enhancement and protection of environmental resources, and promotion of civil and labor rights. These are areas that affect the quality of social and civil coexistence in the country, even if they do not belong to welfare policies as they are normally defined.

The nonprofit sector in Italy is made up of:

- private, nonprofit organizations that are aimed at meeting needs of a collective nature;
- organizations that are aimed at meeting the needs of members (such as recreational clubs or sports clubs).

Both types of organizations are worth considering as it is difficult to draw a clear line between the interest of the community and the interest of a group. Moreover, organizations that defend and pursue the interest of their members represent important contributions to the social fabric of the country.

The Italian nonprofit sector presents itself as a still undefined universe, positioned in the undefined area created by the overlapping sets of public and private institutions. Based on 2019 ISTAT data, nonprofit institutions in Italy are 362,634 and employ 861,919 people. Over the years, both the number of organizations and the number of employees have increased (+0.9% and +1%). The main organizational types (note: ISTAT (2019), structure and profiles of the nonprofit sector, 2019) are:

- volunteer organizations: "Third sector entity established in an associative form that carries out activities in the general interest, mainly for the benefit of third parties, relying predominantly on the voluntary work of its members. Voluntary organizations were introduced into the Italian legal system by Framework Law No.

266/1991 subsequently abolished by Legislative Decree 117/2017 (Art. 102). However, until the Single National Register of the Third Sector becomes fully operational, the previous rules continue to apply to entities registered in the regional registers of volunteer organizations (Art. 101, Legislative Decree No. 117/2017 and subsequent circulars on the matter issued by the Ministry of Labor and Social Policy)";

• associations of social promotion: "A third sector entity established in the form of an association, for the purpose of carrying out in favor of its members, their family members or third parties one or more activities of general interest, making use mainly of the voluntary activity of its members. Organizations for social promotion were introduced into the Italian legal system by Framework Law No. 383/2000 subsequently abolished by Legislative Decree No. 117/2017 (Art. 102). However, until the Single National Register of the Third Sector becomes fully operational, the previous rules continue to apply to entities registered in the registers of social promotion associations (Art. 101, Legislative Decree No. 117/2017 and subsequent circulars on the matter issued by the Ministry of Labor and Social Policy)";

• social business: "A third-sector entity that carries out on a stable and principal basis a business activity in the general interest, on a non-profit basis and for civic, solidarity and socially useful purposes. The case of social business is regulated by Legislative Decree No. 112 of July 3, 2017, which abolished Legislative Decree No. 155/2006. Social cooperatives and their consortia, referred to in Law No. 381 of November 8, 1991, acquire by right the status of social businesses (Art. 1 co. 4, Legislative Decree No. 112/2017)";

• ONLUS: "Private entity (association, committee, foundation, cooperative society and other entity of a private nature) established with the exclusive pursuit of social solidarity purposes and for carrying out activities in one or more of the following areas: social and socio-health assistance, health care, charity, education, training, amateur sports, protection, promotion and enhancement of matters of artistic and historical interest, protection and enhancement of nature and the environment, promotion of culture and art, protection of civil rights, scientific research (Art. 10, Legislative Decree No. 460/1997). The articles of Legislative Decree No. 460/1997 that governed the recognition of non-profit status were abolished by Legislative Decree No. 117/2017 (Art. 102). Until the Single National Register of the Third Sector is fully operational and the tax period following the European Commission's authorization of the new tax regime, the previous rules continue to apply to entities registered in the Onlus registry (Art. 101, Legislative Decree No. 117/2017 and subsequent circulars on the matter issued by the Ministry of Labor and Social Policy)";

- social cooperatives: "Third-sector entity in the form of a cooperative company founded with the purpose of supporting human promotion and social and labor integration of citizens belonging to the so-called disadvantaged and weak categories (former prisoners, the disabled, single mothers, etc.). It is established and governed by Framework Law No. 381/1991, which distinguishes social cooperatives according to its purpose: type A, if they pursue the general interest of the community in human promotion and social integration through the management of social, health and educational services; type B, if they carry out agricultural, industrial, commercial or service activities aimed at the employment of disadvantaged people. Social cooperatives acquire by right the status of social business under Legislative Decree No. 112/2017";
- foundations: "Private non-profit institution, endowed with its own assets, involved in multiple areas: assistance, education, scientific research, disbursement of prizes and awards, training, and so on. Its regulation is provided for in the Civil Code and the legal structure may vary depending on the type of foundation that is established, and it is optional to apply for recognition under Presidential Decree 361/2000 through registration in the Register of Legal Persons, established at the Territorial Government Offices (UTG former prefectures). [Articles 14 et seq. of the Civil Code; Presidential Decree No. 361/2000]";
- other institutions.

In the Italian context, it is appropriate to adopt a broad definition of nonprofit among the definitions proposed in Section 1.8. According to Salamon and Anheier, a company belonging to the nonprofit sector is identified when the following criteria are met (Salamon & Anheier, 1994):

a   formal incorporation;
b   private legal nature;
c   self-governance, structural, and organizational autonomy;
d   absence of profit allocation;
e   presence of a certain degree of volunteer labor.

1.9.1 Formal incorporation

The company must be formally incorporated and have a statute or otherwise a document regulating the members' access, their behavior and mutual relations, proving organizational consistency and stability over time.

1.9.2 Private legal nature

The nonprofit organization should not be part of the public sector, although in practice the boundary between public and private is difficult to identify (Barbetta et al., 1993). First, the phenomenon of privatization is also beginning to affect the nonprofit sector, with the effect that organizations that are now part of the public sector could become nonprofits. Second, the concept of public and private are the subject of doctrinal debate among jurists. In addition, there are entities that are qualified by law as "subject of public interest" and cases of organizations whose nature is not easy to define. The private legal nature must therefore be carefully investigated by understanding the will or inclinations that are prevalent in the legal system.

1.9.3 Self-governance, structural, and organizational autonomy

The organization must not be controlled in the execution of decision-making processes by other organizations belonging to the public sector or the business sector.

In order to verify compliance with this requirement, it is possible to analyze the composition of the boards of directors: if individuals appointed by public or corporate entities represent the majority, we cannot speak of a nonprofit organization.

The organization must also possess identity and independence based on the input of entrepreneurship, capital, labor, knowledge, skills, and technology in a manner capable of lasting over time, within the framework of an economic-financial balance, understood as a balance of a dynamic type aimed at the creation and not the destruction of resources, and of a social type, aimed at the creation and not the destruction of consensus.

1.9.4 Absence of "profit" allocation

The organization's purpose is not to achieve a positive operating result. In the event that it does achieve it is required to invest it in the business. In any case, the distribution of income to both members and employees shall be prohibited.

The purpose of the nonprofit organization is to create social utility, collective benefits, and not to increase income to be shared among those who govern and lead the organization.

In carrying out the activity, a "surplus" may be realized resulting from the efficient and innovative use of available resources or due to the difference between revenues/contributions and costs of obtaining the goods and services whose production activity is aimed at. This surplus cannot be appropriated by those who have some ownership over the organization, but it must be reinvested for the survival, development, and qualification of the organization itself, considered as an entity intended to last over time (Caselli, 1996).

Sometimes, however, the guise of the nonprofit organization is employed for purposes that, while not being directly profit-oriented, are so in a mediated way. Therefore, for example, foundations created for the sole purpose of holding a majority share in the capital of companies or groups cannot be considered nonprofit organizations. In this case, we can observe an instrumental use of the legal form of a nonprofit organization, motivated by reasons that do not pertain to the charitable spirit of the foundation but perhaps have the sole purpose of making possible scale-ups difficult or paying less tax.

1.9.5 Presence of volunteer labor

Volunteers may hold any role within the organization, whether operational or managerial functions, or activity guidance. The presence of volunteer activities can also be identified when salaries below the market average for homogeneous professional positions are present.

Using the above definition, the sector that emerges includes:

* organizations that primarily pursue the interest of their members such as sports associations or members-only recreational clubs;
* as well as organizations aimed at improving the living conditions of individuals outside the organization or more generally at the welfare of the entire community such as many volunteer organizations.

The line between the two groups of organizations is very difficult to identify because the same organization can carry out activities with the aim of pursuing the interests of its members and activities aimed at the collective welfare. Think, for example, of a sports association that seeks to create recreational and meeting opportunities for members, however, at the same time fulfills the task of carrying out a preventive action against juvenile delinquency (Barbetta et al., 1993).

It also turns out to be very difficult to define the concept of "community welfare". It is a concept that varies over time and space. The concept of welfare is related to the era we refer to and the place we take into consideration. Moreover, it's a subjective concept. Therefore, the cultural, ideological, economic, and religious context influences the definition of this concept. Organizations that engage in political and religious activities are also to be considered nonprofits. Political activity means any activity aimed at influencing the outcome of an electoral campaign. Religious activity means any worship activity. It is rather difficult to give a definition; the one used tries to mediate between the need to focus attention on organizations most likely to be of some economic significance and the need not to overlook economic realities that are insignificant but no less important in national social and cultural contexts. The criteria used have the advantage of flexibility and generality and therefore can be interpreted and used in different contexts.

In the following chapters we will consider a broad definition of a nonprofit organization by considering, however, the universe of only those companies that develop, directly or even indirectly, a productive activity. Production need not necessarily be expressed in measurable units of products or services.

1.10 The third sector

The first EU definition of the third sector dates back to 1978 ("A Project for Europe"). This term refers to the set of private, nonbusiness, and nonprofit organizations that produce services – defined as socially useful – that private sector companies (first sector) could not produce, due to the impossibility of achieving economically viable conditions, and that the public sector (second sector) does not produce due to lack of resources or initiative or institutional interest. It therefore includes private companies acting in different sectors. In Italy, official recognition of the third sector occurred in 2016 (Delegated Law 106 of 2016) and subsequently with the publication of the Code of the Third Sector (Legislative Decree 117/2017). The latter lists entities that are part of the third sector: "volunteer organizations, associations for social promotion, philanthropic entities, social enterprises, including social cooperatives, associative networks, mutual aid societies, associations, recognized or unrecognized, foundations and other entities of a private nature other than companies constituted for the pursuit, on a non-profit basis of civic, solidaristic and socially useful purposes by carrying out, exclusively or principally, one or more activities of general interest in the form of voluntary action or free disbursement of money, goods or services, or in the form of mutual aid, or the production or exchange of goods or services, and registered in the single national register of the Third Sector". Sometimes the third sector is considered a nonprofit sector. In reality, in order to become a third sector entity, it is necessary to comply with a number of requirements that sometimes nonprofit bodies do not meet (carrying out activities in the general interest, being registered in the single national register of the third sector). In addition, some nonprofit organizations are excluded from the third sector by legislative provision (trade unions, parties, banking foundations). This research focuses on nonprofits in general (whether or not they are part of the third sector).

Notes

1 We define the economic stakeholder as "the person or group of persons whose predominant interest guides the administration of the organization. The economic entity can only dominate the administration when it has in effect the capacity and ability to govern it and direct it in every area in the ways and for the purposes deemed advantageous" (Zappa, 1956, p. 86).

See also Mella (1992, pp. 117–119) where corporate stakeholders are defined as "the set of natural or legal persons who enable the existence of a given company or who obtain economic benefits from it". Corporate stakeholders are distinguished into legal entity, formally responsible for the activity of the company; operational entity, which in fact develops the business activity; and economic entity, which benefits from the results of that activity. The economic stakeholder is defined as "the set of natural persons in whose predominant interest the company is set up and carries out its activities; that is, the set of persons who bear institutional interests in the company" (Farneti, 2000, p. 16).

2 The strand of studies on corporate social responsibility has long highlighted the need for tools to inform different stakeholders on the degree to which their expectations are being met and to examine the externalities produced by corporate activities. There are many contributions on this, including Nardo & Siboni, 2018; Arvidson & Lyon, 2014; Mussari & Monfardini, 2010.

References

Abramson, A. J. (1986). *Nonprofit sector and the new federal budget*. The Urban Institute Press.

Airoldi, G., (1996). *Le aziende nonprofit: Definizioni e classificazioni, within Le aziende non profit tra stato e mercato*. Bologna: Clueb.

Airoldi, G., Brunetti, G., & Coda, V. (2020). *Corso di economia aziendale*. Bologna: Il mulino.

Anthony, R. N., & Young, D. W. (1988). *Management control in non-profit organizations*. Illinois: IRWIN, Homewood.

Arvidson, M., & Lyon, F. (2014). Social impact measurement and non-profit organisations: Compliance, resistance, and promotion. *VOLUNTAS: International Journal of Voluntary and Nonprofit Organizations, 25*(4), 869–886.

Barbetta, G. P., Anheier, H. K., Hwang, C., & Salamon, L. M. (1993). *Defining the nonprofit sector: Italy*. Johns Hopkins Institute for Policy Studies.

Bassanini, M. C., & Ranci, P. (1990). Non per profitto. Il settore dei soggetti che erogano servizi di interesse collettivo senza fine di lucro. *Milán: Fondazione A. Olivetti. La especificidad organizativa del tercer sector: Tipos y dinámicas Papers, 56*(1998), 193.

Capaldo, P. (1996). *Le aziende non profit: definizioni e classificazioni. Aa. Vv., Le aziende non profit tra stato e mercato*. Bologna: Atti del convegno Aidea, Clueb.

Caselli, L. (1996). *La produzione e la distribuzione di valore*. Bologna: Atti del Convegno Aidea, Le aziende non profit fra Stato e Mercato, Clueb.

Cavenago, D. (1996). *Dirigere e governare una organizzazione non profit: economia & management*. Padova: Cedam.

Cestari, J. M. A. P., Tavares Treinta, F., Francis Moura, L., Munik, J., Pinheiro de Lima, E., Deschamps, F., ... & Duarte, R. (2021). The characteristics of nonprofit performance measurement systems. *Total Quality Management & Business Excellence*, 1–31.

Civitillo, R., Ricci, P., & Simonetti, B. (2019). Management and performance of Non-Profit Institutions: Finding new development trajectories – evidence from Italy. *Quality & Quantity, 53*(5), 2275–2290.

Cutt, J., & Murray, V. (2013). *Accountability and effectiveness evaluation in nonprofit organizations*. Routledge.

Davis, P. S., & Pett, T. L. (2002). Measuring organizational efficiency and effectiveness. *Journal of Management Research, 2*(2), 87.

Farneti, G. (2000). *Il bilancio dell'ente locale: Determinazioni preventive e consuntive*. Giappichelli, Torino.

Ferrero, G. (1968). *Istituzioni di economia d'azienda*. Milano: Giuffrè.

Ghani, E. K., Said, J., & Yusuf, S. N. S. (2012). Service quality measurement tool in Islamic nonprofit organizations: An urgent need. *International Business and Management, 5*(2), 71–75.

Guatri, L. (1997). *Valore e intangibles nella misura della performance aziendale: Un percorso storico* (p. 218). Milano: Egea.

Hansman, H. B. (1986). The role of nonprofit enterprise. In S. Rose-Ackerman (Ed.), *The economics of nonprofit institutions. Studies in structure and policy* (pp. 57–84). Oxford/New York: Oxford University Press.

Hatzfeld, C. A. (2014). Performance measurement in nonprofit organizations – Exploring the commonalities among impact, outcome, and performance measurement in open youth service providers. *International Journal of Management Cases, 16*(4), 76–92.

Hoque, Z., & Parker, L. (Eds.). (2018). *Performance management in nonprofit organizations: Global perspectives*. Routledge.

Laurett, R., & Ferreira, J. J. (2018). Strategy in nonprofit organizations: A systematic literature review and agenda for future research. *VOLUNTAS: International Journal of Voluntary and Nonprofit Organizations, 29*(5), 881–897.

Lyons, M. (2020). *Third sector: The contribution of nonprofit and cooperative enterprise in Australia.* Routledge.

Mason, R. O., & Swanson, E. B. (1988). *Gli indici di valutazione per le decisioni aziendali. Amigoni F. (a cura di), Misurazioni d'azienda.* Milano: Giuffré.

Medina-Borja, A., & Triantis, K. (2007). A conceptual framework for evaluating the performance of nonprofit social service organizations. *International Journal of Technology Management, 37*(1–2), 147–161.

Mella, P. (1992). *Economia Aziendale.* Torino: Utet.

Mella, P. (1993). *Contabilità e bilancio.* Torino: Utet.

Mella, P. (1997). *Dai Sistemi al pensiero sistemico: Per capire i sistemi e pensare con i sistemi* (Vol. 28). Milano: FrancoAngeli.

Mella, P. (2008). Systems Thinking e System Dynamics. L'arte di capire la dinamica ed il controllo dei sistemi. *Economia Aziendale 2000 Web (ISSN:1826-4719), 4/2008,* 153–192.

Mella, P. (2012). *Systems thinking. intelligence in action.* New York, Dordrecht, London: Springer.

Mella, P. (2014). *Teoria del controllo. Dal systems thinking ai sistemi di controllo* (pp. 1–408). Milano: Franco Angeli.

Mella, P. (2017). The unexpected cybernetics life of collectivities. The combinatory systems approach. *Kybernetes, 46*(7), 1086–1111.

Mella, P. (2021a, 1st Ed. 2014). *The magic ring. systems thinking approach to control systems* (Second Edition). Switzerland: Springer Nature.

Mella, P. (2021b). Entrepreneurial dynamics and clusters formation. The combinatory systems view. *Economia Aziendale Online, 12*(1), 99–124.

Mella, P. (2021c). *Aziende: Istituzioni di economia aziendale.* FrancoAngeli.

Mella, P. (2022). Global warming: Is it (im)possible to stop it? The systems thinking approach. *Energies, 15*(705), 1–33.

Mella P., & Gazzola P. (2019). Improving managers' intelligence through systems thinking. *Kybernetes, 48*(1), 58–78.

Mella, P., & Rangone, A. (2019). Obstacles to managing dynamic systems. The systems thinking approach. *International Journal of Business and Social Science, 10*(8), 24–41.

Micheli, P., & Kennerley, M. (2005). Performance measurement frameworks in the public and nonprofit sectors. *Production Planning & Control, 16*(2), 125–134.

Molteni, M. M. (1990). *Alle origini di concezioni innovative di impresa.* Milano: Egea.

Moura, L. F., de Lima, E. P., Deschamps, F., Van Aken, E., da Costa, S. E. G., Treinta, F. T., & Cestari, J. M. A. P. (2019). Designing performance measurement systems in nonprofit and public administration organizations. *International Journal of Productivity and Performance Management, 68*(8), 1373–1410.

Mouzas, S. (2006). Efficiency versus effectiveness in business networks. *Journal of business research, 59*(10-11), 1124–1132.

Mussari, R., & Monfardini, P. (2010). Practices of social reporting in public sector and non-profit organizations: An Italian perspective. *Public Management Review, 12*(4), 487–492.

Nardo, M. T., & Siboni, B. (2018). Requirements and practices of social reporting in Italian not-for-profit organisations. In R. Tench, B. Jones, & W. Sun (Eds.). The critical state of corporate social responsibility in Europe (Critical studies on corporate responsibility, governance and sustainability, Vol. 12). Bingley: Emerald Publishing Limited, 299–317.

Onida, P. (1961). Economicita', socialita'ed efficienza nell'amministrazione d'impresa. Casa ed. della "Rivista italiana di ragioneria", n. 3–4, p. 57.

Poister, T. H. (2003). *Measuring performance in public and nonprofit organizations.* John Wiley & Sons.

Poister, T. H., Aristigueta, M. P., & Hall, J. L. (2014). *Managing and measuring performance in public and nonprofit organizations: An integrated approach.* John Wiley & Sons.

Powell, W. W. (1987) (ed.). *The nonprofit sector.* A Research Handbook, Yale University Press.

Salamon, L. M., & Anheier, H. K. (1994). Measuring the non-profit sector cross-nationally: A comparative methodology. *Voluntas: International Journal of Voluntary and Nonprofit Organizations, 4*(4), 530–554.

Salamon, L. M., & Anheier, H. K. (1992). Toward an understanding of the international nonprofit sector: The Johns Hopkins Comparative Nonprofit Sector Project. *Nonprofit Management and Leadership, 2*(3), 311–324.

ISTAT (2019), structure and profiles of the nonprofit sector, 2019. https://www.istat.it/it/archivio/262507

Superti Furga, F. (1971). *Osservazioni sulla logica operativa dei sistemi aziendali integrati.* Milano: Giuffrè.

Terzo, G., Notarstefano, G., & Di Maggio, U. (2022). Non-profit sector and regional well-being in Italy. *Regional Studies,* 1–16.

Tessitore, A. (1996). *La produzione e la distribuzione del valore. Le aziende non profit tra Stato e Mercato.* CLUEB.

Treinta, F. T., Moura, L. F., Almeida Prado Cestari, J. M., Pinheiro de Lima, E., Deschamps, F., Gouvea da Costa, S. E., … & Leite, L. R. (2020). Design and implementation factors for performance measurement in non-profit organizations: A literature review. *Frontiers in Psychology, 1799,* 1–14.

Velli, V., & Sirakoulis, K. (2018). Performance measurement in nonprofit theater organizations: The case of Greek municipal and regional theaters. *International Journal of Arts Management, 21*(1), 49–60.

Zappa, G. (1927). *Tendenze nuove negli studi di ragioneria: discorso inaugurale dell'anno accademico 1926–27 nel R. Istituto superiore di scienze economiche e commerciali di Venezia.* SA Istituto editoriale scientifico.

Zappa, G. (1956). *Le produzioni nell'economia delle imprese: tomo primo.* Milano: Giuffrè.

2 Nonprofit Organizations in Systemic Theory

2.1 Nonprofit organizations as open systems[1]

Every organization, or system (Galassi & Mattessich, 2004; Rusconi, 2019; Zappa, 1937, 1956), can be thought of as embedded within a macrosystem, or environment from which the system is distinguished by a boundary. A system for which it is relevant to consider that there are inputs and/or outputs with the environment referred to as open. Open systems can be classified into physical, biological, and social. Social open systems are those identified in the observation of social structures such as an organization. The organization can thus be considered an open (Bertini, 1988; Contrafatto & Rusconi, 2005; Ferrero, 1987; Paolone & D'Amico, 1994; Signori & Rusconi, 2009) social system (Amaduzzi, 1967; Coronella et al., 2018; Superti Furga, 1971), of a socio-technical nature, that is, a human-machine system featuring elements whose state depends partly on technical operations and partly on human decisions.

The characteristics of an open system are:

- the organization, which creates order and consistency of behavior, allows structures to win out over the chaotic fluctuation of the environment;
- the maintenance of the structure or teleonomy, that is, the preservation over time of the system structure, even as the components of the system change; we define teleonomy as the aptitude of an open system to maintain the "structural blueprint" even as the elements that make up the structure change, keeping itself active in the environment, in the macrosystem of which it is a part; we define autopoiesis as the process by which the system changes its elements reproducing itself over time;

DOI: 10.4324/9781003350439-3

- the adaptability, organizations are dynamic systems that set in motion a spatial and/or temporal evolution that manifests itself as a change in internal states;
- the control;
- equifinality, which is the ability of systems to achieve a goal despite starting from different initial states.

2.2 The maintenance of the structure

Open systems have a structure that distinguishes them with respect to the environment. An open system is a separable object with respect to the macrosystem, a system boundary can be identified so that the elements inside and outside the system can be observed. Open systems are characterized by the preservation of the structure of the system over time, even as the components of the system change. The structure of the system can be regarded as deriving from a structural or teleonomic design, which may be the result of the coordinated action of chance and necessity or resulting from a purposeful design of a subject devising the structure. The ability of a system to maintain itself active over a period of time T – even if it is composed of elements that have an average life of less than that period T – is related to the structural organization of the system. The design of the structure is accomplished through the invariant structure, which is composed of elements that receive a precise functional allocation within the structure and that can transmit, to new components, information about the location they are to occupy. Individual components may vary, but thanks to the information the structure is preserved.

The aptitude of an open system to maintain its structural design despite the component variation is called teleonomy. Teleonomy allows a system to keep itself alive in the environment of which it is a part.

We can further distinguish between exogenous and endogenous teleonomy:

- exogenous, such as the environment's aptitude to preserve systems that the environment considers useful;
- endogenous, such as the system's ability to maintain its structure (Mella, 1992, pp. 50–51).

Open systems are also dynamic systems that evolve in space and time; teleonomic behavior leads the system to respond to environmental changes in order to continuously adapt to varied conditions until the initial structure changes. These are self-regulating systems. Once generated, by using external resources, they carry out processes designed to regenerate the system structure over time, keeping the organization unaltered.

Their behavior can be described:

- from an internal point of view;
- from an external point of view.

From an internal point of view it can be seen as a network of micro processes that recursively generate the elements needed to produce the organs that develop the process network. From an external point of view, it can be examined as a succession of macro processes by which the system unit selects energy and instrumental inputs from the environment in order to preserve the process network.

2.3 Control in a dynamic system

Such systems also develop a control that allows the system to be able to act on its states in order to produce desired behaviors. A programmed dynamic can be considered by an external observer as a behavioral goal that can be ascribed to an open system. The system can be controlled if it can be forced to produce actual dynamics that are in accordance with the predetermined behavioral goal (Mella, 1997). A system is defined as instrumental if it is externally controlled for the pursuit of the goals of some other system of which it is thus an instrument. A self-controlled, noninstrumental system is defined as cybernetic in that it possesses goals that it is able to pursue with a self-control system. If a system is cybernetic and, at the same time, it sets its own goals, it can be referred to as teleological.

2.4 Organizations as transformation systems

A transformation system (Mella, 2012b) occurs when it makes sense to think of the task performed as a transformation, intended in the broadest sense, of objects entering the system, the inputs, and different objects leaving the system, the outputs. Transformation systems implement transformations on elements coming from the environment; the inputs are elements that come into contact with the structure; the outputs are represented by those same inputs after undergoing transformation (Ashby, 1964). A transformation system will always have inputs and outputs and will be of the kind in Figure 2.1.

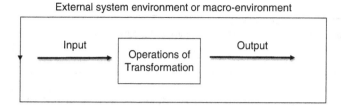

External system environment or macro-environment

Figure 2.1 The organization as a transformation system.

Among the many interesting classifications of transformation systems, it is possible to characterize them, in relation to input and output dimensions, into modal transformers and quantitative transformers. Modal transformation systems are those for which it makes sense to consider inputs and outputs only in qualitative terms. The transformation alters the state of qualitative input dimensions. Outputs result from changes in the input modality. Quantitative transformation systems are metrizable systems, those for which it makes sense to consider inputs and outputs in terms of quantitative dimensions.

Any transformation system is defined open if:

1 inputs come from the outside, that is, from the environment;
2 the outputs return to the outside, that is, from the environment;
3 some of the inputs remain within the system for some time to form the operational structure by which to implement the transformations and, in some cases, to increase the size of the system.

Nonprofit organizations can be interpreted as open systems of transformation that implement in parallel and in coordination, with four fundamental transformations: productive, economic, financial, and managerial, which will be analyzed in the following sections.

2.5 The productive transformation

Productive transformation (Mella, 2021a; Gazzola & Mella, 2012) is a utility transformation: production factors having a given utility[2] are transformed into products – capable of delivering greater utility – and eventually into residuals. By analyzing different types of organizations and analyzing different production combinations, it is easy to notice the similarities. It is therefore possible to generalize the notion of a productive transformation system. If we indicate with QF

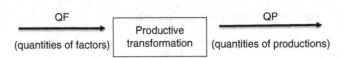

Figure 2.2 The productive transformation.

the quantities of factors employed in productions and with QP the quantities of productions sold, we can represent the productive transformation (Figure 2.2).

In nonprofit organizations, the term production is to be understood in a broad sense, that is, as the production of goods or services that satisfy needs, wants, aspirations (Capaldo, 1996). In nonprofit organizations that allocate production to predetermined subjects (Figure 2.3), a few production process hypotheses can be identified:

a   the production of goods or services with divisible demands that are provided to individual subjects according to their specific demand. This is the case with organizations that run training centers, sports facilities, medical centers, welfare and assistance companies for different professional groups, etc.;

b   the production of goods or services of indivisible demands that are provided generically and indiscriminately to all members. This is the case with trade associations between companies operating in

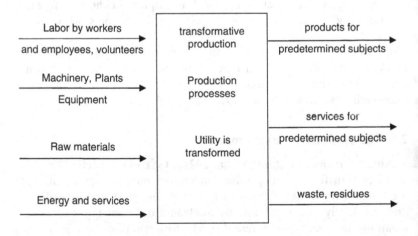

Figure 2.3 Productive transformation in nonprofit organizations that allocate production to predetermined subjects.

the same sector that aims at collecting, processing, and disseminating information concerning the sector to which they belong and defending, if necessary, the interests of the category itself; also included in this category are services provided by companies established to promote and disseminate the use of their products through various concerted actions;

c   the production of goods or services that are in part indivisible in demand and thus made available to all members, and in part divisible and thus provided to individuals at their request. This is the case with trade associations, which, aside from carrying out a generic activity aimed at looking after the interests of the entire category, also offer a consulting service to individual companies.

In nonprofit provider organizations, the production process is aimed at the provision of services – in the areas of culture, health care, assistance, scientific research, etc. – to determined individuals living in disadvantaged conditions, or more generally to the entire community. It is based on the voluntary free commitment of people moved by philanthropic, religious, cultural, etc. intentions who come together for a common commitment aimed at the realization of a unified project. This organization, while remaining in the private sphere, is aimed at achieving socially useful goals.

The production process (Figure 2.4) employs as inputs various goods, materials, food commodities, etc., which are normally derived

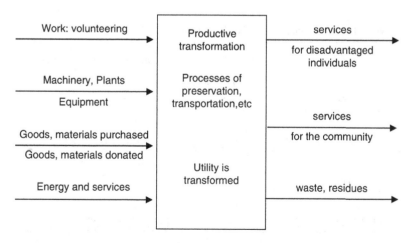

Figure 2.4 Productive transformation in nonprofit provider organization.

from donations; particularly important are the services of free labor that are commonly referred to as volunteer work. This is especially the case when these nonprofit organizations offer goods and services for which there is no need for complex facilities and special assets, but rather the availability of qualified personnel such as doctors, psychologists, lawyers, skilled workers, etc.

Social companies produce goods or services intended for the market. However, they are aimed at:

- creating jobs for disadvantaged individuals who otherwise would not be able to take part in the normal production process that the state or businesses do not offer;
- offering useful or necessary goods and services that the state and businesses do not offer.

These companies operate in sectors and in ways that businesses do not take into consideration as they would not allow the implementation of an economics-based management rationale. Their missions can be traced to the general or social interest, with strong ethical drives. They are mainly based on volunteer work. Thus, disadvantaged workers are paired with volunteer workers to monitor and improve the services offered to customers (Figure 2.5).

Productive transformation should not only be considered as transformation of factors into quantitatively defined outputs. Consideration

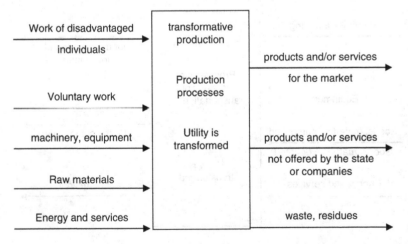

Figure 2.5 Productive transformation in nonprofit social organizations.

must also be given to the quality of the productions obtained.[3] We do not consider the quality of the factors employed as a variable that cannot be controlled by the organization. We can complete the definition of productive transformation by considering it as the transformation observed in companies as transformers of factors into quantitatively and qualitatively defined productions.[4]

2.6 The economic transformation

The concept of "production" as the qualifying element of nonprofit companies is certainly not appropriate to explain their formation and development. Nonprofit organizations are not just production companies, considering that the production stage acquires economic meaning and value only in the presence of a defined system of exchanges, within which emerges the allocation of the wealth produced. In companies, in general, it is therefore possible to identify another kind of transformation: that between values (Mella, 1979). When inputs are purchased, there are costs involved, which, from an economic standpoint, represent the value attributed to the inputs purchased. When you transfer the obtained outputs or provide services you earn revenues which, from an economic perspective, represent the value attributed to the transferred outputs (Mella, 1992). Thus, it is possible to identify an economic transformation (Canziani, 2007) of costs into revenues. If we assume, for simplicity's sake, that companies cannot purchase factors in excess with respect to demands, and that the quantities of factors involved in the production process are bought on the market at their purchase price pP. Suppose that there is no such thing as the issue of inventories of end goods and that all quantities produced are sold in the market at their selling price pS. Let's denote with pP the purchase prices of the factors and with pS the selling prices of the productions and add these values as the inputs of the productive transformation system, the latter turns into the economic transformation system (Figure 2.6). By multiplying the quantities of the factors used in production and their prices, we determine the costs of the factors used in production, indicated in the figure by the symbol CF.

Figure 2.6 The organization as an economic transformer.

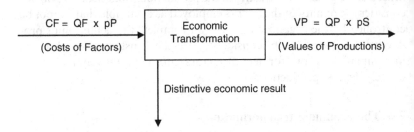

Figure 2.7 The organization as an economic transformer.

Similarly, by multiplying the quantities of the productions sold and their prices, we determine the sales values of the factors used to produce, indicated in the figure by the symbol VP.

The distinctive economic result can be considered the derived output of the previous model, which can be rewritten in Figure 2.7.

What has been observed in general can be applied to the production processes carried out by nonprofit organizations. These processes, in turn, are also subject to economic evaluations to avoid sub-optimizing the use of resources for the benefit of those to whom the company is directed.

Therefore, nonprofit organizations as economic transformers turn costs into revenues.

Costs can be grouped into two major categories:

- costs for the survival, or management costs;
- costs to fulfill the purposes, or institutional costs.

Positive income components arising from the production process can be summarized as follows:

- "prices" in the general sense of remunerative fees for services;
- "contributions", in the sense of remunerative consideration to partially cover the cost of services;
- "membership fees", paid broadly to use the services of the nonprofit organization;
- "subsidies", intended as contributions not related to the services.

Subsidies may be contributed by individuals to help cover negative income components in various forms, or by the state.

From the difference between the positive components of income and the related costs of the factors used to obtain the goods sold or services

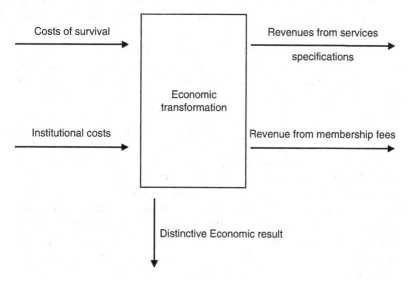

Figure 2.8 The nonprofit organization as an economic transformer.

rendered arises the distinctive economic result. From the difference between the positive components and the management costs arises the share allocable to the accomplishment of the purposes. In general, the economic transformation of nonprofit organizations will look as in Figure 2.8.

Returning to the classification of nonprofit organizations based on the ability by the beneficiaries of the production to cover the costs seen as the ability to achieve positive income components necessary to adequately remunerate all the factors of production, covering all the negative components, we can distinguish the economic transformation of different types of organizations.

Economically self-sufficient nonprofit organizations are expected to cover all costs with the membership fees paid by their associates. Economically non-self-sufficient nonprofit companies will cover costs according to a varied mix of positive income components. With regard to private subsidies, those from the voluntary sector and foundations are of particular importance.

2.7 The reference value system

The evaluation of economic transformation is basically similar to companies, what changes profoundly is the system of reference values and thus with it changes the way of appreciating the cost-effectiveness of productions (Tessitore, 1996). The wide variety of nonprofit organizations cannot be brought back to a unified model of operation; however, it is possible to identify some common elements. The broad range of nonprofit organizations is characterized by the limited economic significance undertaken by the exchange value system, both on the purchasing side of the factors of production and on the selling side of the goods produced or services rendered. The values formed around the scheduled productions carried out by nonprofit organizations sometimes reflect the efficient market conditions, but at other times they represent the added value produced; that is, produced and distributed at the same time (e.g., free or otherwise unprofitable services), at other times they highlight the income to be allocated to parties other than those who provided capital and labor. In such a diverse context, the exchange value system does not always represent the cost-effectiveness of management. The reasons for the convenience of operating economically are to be found in a "system of inequalities" whereby the marginal productivity of the factors employed, expressed in value, must be greater than their respective market values, and the value of the production carried out must be greater than the marginal costs valued at market prices. According to classical utility theory, it is necessary to show a surplus of the use-value over the exchange or appraisal value, under market conditions, of the factors acquired and to show a surplus of the exchange or appraisal value, under market conditions, of the products over the use-value of the factors employed. In the case of the nonexistence of an efficient system of negotiated prices for both the purchase of production factors and the sale of productions, it is possible to use as a reference the current values determined in relation to the most advantageous prices that the market situation permits.

The objectives of nonprofit organizations are to help remedy the deficiencies and reduce the imbalances created by modern economic and social systems, to spread wealth, to create new employment opportunities, and to provide goods or services to individuals unable to access them through the market or inadequately protected by state interventions. They often operate through the free support of volunteers and the payment of lower fees than those recognized by the market for the provision of similar productive factors. Sometimes consumers are willing to pay higher than market prices with the aim of favoring certain categories of people or enabling the development of areas that are socially in need of support.

The presence of volunteers and the interventions of the public administration allow to reduce the "convenience deficit" to undertake certain productive activities, making economically viable some initiatives that, according to market parameters, would be judged uneconomic (Tessitore, 1996). Despite the market access barriers, nonprofit organizations are put in a position to operate, so they are required to carry out the production process according to the paradigm of cost-effectiveness. Reducing the level of marginal productivity of factors employed would not be consistent with the nature of a business, just as systematically selling products at prices below the actual marginal cost of production would not be consistent. The differential nature between a business and a nonprofit organization – which emerges not at the production process level, but at the allocation level of the "social surplus", intended as the management outcome – must take into account that the beneficiaries of the business activity achieve a positive surplus, while the people who contribute without remuneration are also willing to accept a negative surplus. Economic efficiency requires that the algebraic sum of surpluses produced and disbursed be maximum. Therefore, economic production is achieved only by those productive combinations that tend to maximize the operating surplus to be allocated to the social groups that gravitate around the organization.

The result of their work must be evaluated not in relation to the increase in wealth, as measured by the contrast of exchange values (price-revenue and price-cost), or by the size of the wealth that can be allocated among those who have contributed to the production, but in relation to the quantity and quality of the needs satisfied, that is, the "utility" produced (Borgonovi, 1996).

2.8 Organizations that allocate production to their members

In nonprofit organizations, whose outputs are intended for members, a self-consumption economy scheme is implemented. The goal they are aimed at is not income generation, but rather the production and consumption of goods by the members (Airoldi, 1996). These companies are united by the characteristic that the resources needed to cover the costs of production are provided by the members, since they are the sole recipients of the production. There is, however, the problem of allocating the costs of production among the members; sometimes the allocation is not dictated solely by an economic rationale, or by power relations, but it can be motivated by mutualistic or solidarity-based intentions that can lead to easing the burden on the economically weaker members. Organizations offering shareable goods and services, their participants pay a "price" for each unit requested; the "price" paid is not a real price because it is not the result of a normal market exchange, it is close to the full cost of production. It can be considered a fee established by mutual agreement among all members in order to obtain income that permits the achievement of economic balance. We can call this "price" a *fee*. This fee is close to the full cost. It does not match it because in practice the calculation is made with reference to time intervals that are not short-term, which may be relative to six months, a year or more. It is not adjusted continuously to reflect changes in the conditions that give rise to it because it would be too complex to calculate, so it is normally preferable to make regular updates to take into account changes in cost that are already present and those that are expected in the future.

Sometimes more complex methods are used to determine the fees. Other methods employed are:

- method of double fee;
- method based on the guaranteed minimum.

In nonprofit organizations that employ the "double-fee" method:

- members periodically pay a fixed amount that is not dependent on the quantity of goods and services used;
- when they request goods or services they pay a variable amount based on the quantity requested.

Organizations that apply the "guaranteed minimum" method rely on a commitment from members to periodically request a certain quantity of goods or services and pay the corresponding fixed counter-value. Within organizations offering indivisible goods or services, since it is not possible to identify individual demands, each member is required to pay a contribution to cover costs. Whenever possible, parameters are used that express the utility that members gain, even indirectly, from the social activity. Within organizations that offer goods and services that are partly divisible and partly indivisible, in determining the cost-coverage methods by members, the procedure is the same as in the previous two cases, with the peculiarity that the fee mechanisms are more complex. Regardless of the allocation of costs between members, the economic transformation of nonprofit organizations that allocate production to predetermined subjects takes place with a succession of costs and revenues: management costs and costs of achieving the members' goals, which, in turn, must provide the necessary resources. The nonprofit organization incurs costs to produce, but unlike a company, these are not covered through the market, with all the related risks, but rather ensured by the beneficiaries of the production. Expenses affect income, as members are required to provide the resources necessary to cover the expenses. They may decide to dissolve the organization, to leave it, to reduce the activity, but they must always pay, in the forms and manners established, the resources contingent on expenses.

2.9 The "provider organizations"

In this type of nonprofit organization, the production of goods or provision of services is rendered without a direct counter-performance. Sometimes a symbolic counter-performance takes place, with the purpose of reducing the risk of waste connected with the services offered for free. This counter-performance normally does not represent a contribution from which the coverage of expenses can be obtained. The coverage of expenses comes from the resources of the individuals who support the activity by sharing its goals and objectives. These resources can be either physical (goods, materials, food, etc.) or monetary. The main resource is the provision of free labor: volunteer work.

Some nonprofit organizations survive on volunteer service; these are those organizations that do not require complex structures, but need specialized people such as doctors, psychologists, lawyers, etc. In these cases, production is able to have practically negligible costs. The organization will try to have as many volunteers as possible in order to be able to continuously and effectively provide the desired services. In organizations in which volunteering does not play a crucial role, it still turns out to be very important for both economic and extra-economic reasons such as motivation, emotional involvement, etc. Within economic transformation, there is a succession of income and expenses. Income affects expenses, they are the upper limit, since it is not possible to adjust income to expenses. In these organizations, income is by its nature variable. Expenses are divided into two groups, there are expenses that have a rigid character, the reduction of which could jeopardize the existence of the company. Therefore, there are issues in adjusting expenses to income, so it is necessary to carry out a careful investigation to predict what the fixed costs will be and what the level of income stability will be. It is advisable to have, as far as possible, elastic production facilities capable of varying expenditures as income changes.

2.10 The "social organizations"

These companies are also largely dependent on volunteer work. Volunteering fulfills two functions: one that is purely economic, the other that we might call ethical. Being able to reply on the work of volunteers for free, or at least on off-market conditions, allows the nonprofit organization to achieve the following results:

- increase the wages of disadvantaged individuals working there;
- offer goods and services at affordable prices, especially for disadvantaged individuals;
- improve its operations.

From an ethical standpoint, volunteering makes it possible to "humanize" business activity and thus increase its effectiveness. Economic transformation takes the shape of a sequence of costs and revenues.

The acquisition of production factors can take place:

- at costs representing the expression of prices formed in exchange transactions under market conditions;
- paying a lower fee than the current one;
- sometimes for free.

The production sale can take place:

- at market prices through normal exchange transactions;
- below market values that take into account the economically disadvantaged conditions of the buyers, in which case we cannot speak of prices because they are not established according to market mechanisms (Capaldo, 1996).

2.11 The financial transformation

The third transformation to be addressed is the financial transformation that emerges from the consideration that the organization is an investment hub, meaning that:

- some individuals invest financial resources in the organization;
- the organization invests these resources to acquire the factors necessary to implement the productive transformations, it transforms these factors, and transfers the productions.

The following cycle occurs:

monetary capital invested
↓
purchase of factors
↓
productive transformation
↓
transfer of production
↓
monetary capital regained

We can identify an investment hub where financial investments are received and productive investments are carried out. Normally in businesses, investments precede disinvestments, so monetary expenditures corresponding to costs precede monetary income corresponding to revenues. Due to the asynchrony existing between advance payments and deferred earnings, a monetary requirement arises, the magnitude of which is related to the monetary requirement for initial investment. Normally, the monetary requirement represents the measure of investment needed to implement production before the organization is able to earn revenues through which to fund operational factor requirements and recover, via shares, the capital invested in structural factors.

Monetary needs must be covered:

- with capital provided on a risk equity basis (RC) or loan basis (LC), which must be provided by parties external to the system and which must be adequately remunerated;
- with internally produced resources from net or gross self-financing.

Risk capital and loan capital receive remuneration. The former receive eventual to residual remuneration represented by net profit; the latter receive an agreed remuneration by way of interest. In addition to considering the organization as an investment center, it is also possible to consider the organization as a financial transformation system that turns capital into remuneration by way of profit and by way of interest as highlighted in Figure 2.9.

In order to "make a profit" from the invested capital, the organization invests it in the factors necessary to carry out production processes. The sum of the values of these production factors constitutes

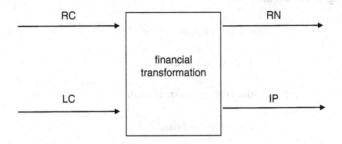

Figure 2.9 The organization as a financial transformer.

the capital invested by the organization and we will refer to it with the symbol IC.[5] If we consider the organization as an investment hub with respect to the invested capital, we can identify a system of funding resources. Therefore we can write the following equation:

$$IC = LC + RC$$

By introducing the invested capital into the previous model, we obtain Figure 2.10.

What has been analyzed for production companies is also valid for nonprofit organizations, with the distinction that the latter:

• can rely on public and private subsidies, in terms of monetary or other types of contributions not related to services (Airoldi, 1996);

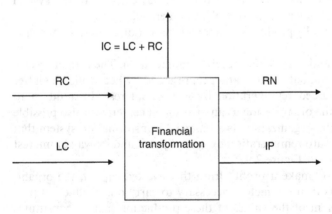

Figure 2.10 The organization as a financial transformer.

- loans payable for consideration often do not exist or play an entirely marginal role;
- we indicate with RC the capital invested by the promoters.

Regarding private subsidies, those from the voluntary sector and foundations are particularly relevant. Foundations fund nonprofit organizations in two different ways:

- by providing subsidies in the form of nonreimbursable monetary contributions;
- by allowing the nonprofit organization, corresponding to the foundation, to have its own capital with the aim of limiting the burdens arising from third-party capital.

Therefore, the previous equation can be rewritten by taking into account the contributions that we will denote by C (Figure 2.11).
  In provider organizations, funding can derive from:

- voluntary contributions;
- transfers from public bodies.

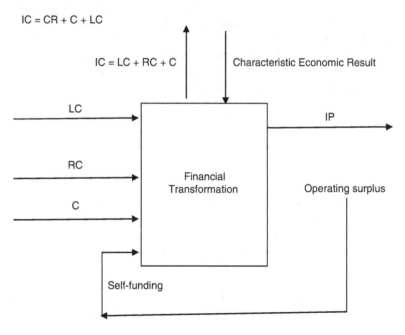

Figure 2.11 The nonprofit organization as a financial transformer.

Voluntary contributions are paid:

a   by subjects who are permanently linked, in some form, to the company; they are normally paid on a regular basis or in any case on the basis of forecasts relating to monetary needs;
b   or by subjects who have no connection with it but who share its goal; they are occasional and are encouraged in various ways, also thanks to "techniques for raising funds in nonprofit organizations".

Transfers from public bodies occur when the purpose of the nonprofit organization has a particular social relevance and is of general interest. They can be granted on a one-off basis or on a continuous basis.

2.12 The managerial transformation

None of the three transformations considered above can be implemented automatically. The intervention of an entity capable of making the necessary decisions is always needed in order for the company to carry out the productive transformation, the economic transformation, and the financial transformation while sustainably maintaining the conditions of endogenous and exogenous teleonomy over time. This subject makes decisions on the basis of the goals set for the organization's activity and the system of information regarding the environment in which the organization operates, taking into account the internal corporate situation and, accepting a given degree of risk, to transform this information into decisions as shown in Figure 2.12.

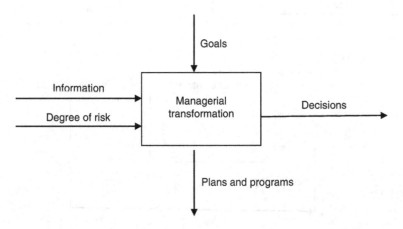

Figure 2.12 Managerial transformation.

In managerial transformation, goals and information are transformed into decisions. Decisions are developed into management plans and programs and become the inputs to the other three transformations, as schematized in Figure 2.13. It thus represents the apex of the other three transformations since none of them can be implemented without the management operations that result from the decisions. Nonprofit organizations, by virtue of their distinctive characteristics, have a greater degree of freedom on the political-administrative level than companies. In fact, they have complete availability over the resources produced and can therefore focus their attention on the management of objectives. In order to identify the objectives, it is necessary to specify that the organization's activity is aimed at satisfying the needs and expectations of different stakeholders (Coda, 1988), that is, categories of interest bearers, which we can recap in the following classes:

- customers/users both explicit and implicit, taking into account all those who can derive benefit from it;
- initiating subject consisting of the core governing body;
- collaborators, both remunerated ones and the volunteers;
- other parties from which the company receives natural, human, and financial resources that play a decisive role in its survival and development, specifically we consider public and private entities that make contributions to the organization.

In these organizations, conflicts are less likely to arise in the economic subject area because managerialism is of a special kind; it is supposed to be socially enlightened. For the achievement of goals, through managerial transformation, the necessary decision-making calculations are made. These can be:

- technical calculations, concerning productive transformation;
- economic calculations, concerning economic transformation;
- financial calculations, concerning financial transformation.

2.13 The complete model with the four transformations

With managerial transformation, it is possible to complete the model of the nonprofit organization as a system of four transformations (Figure 2.13). Managerial transformation is placed at the top of the other transformations because none of the others can be implemented without the management operations that result from the decisions that constitute the output of managerial transformation. Figure 2.13 shows

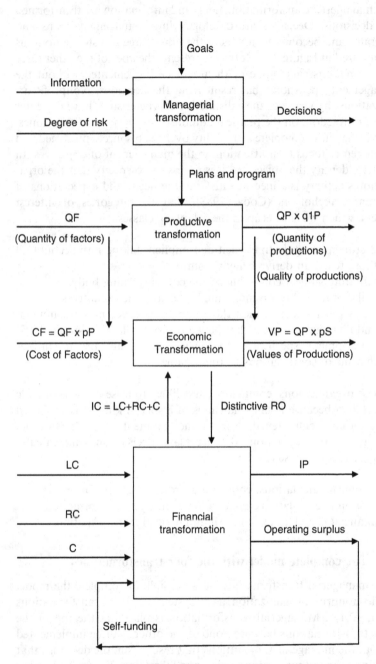

Figure 2.13 The nonprofit organization model as a transformation system.

that the goals represent a fundamental element of managerial transformation; without this information, the other decisions cannot be made. It therefore appears necessary to look further into the analysis of the nonprofit organization's objectives, which underlie decisions, a topic that will be covered in Section 5.3.

2.14 Nonprofit organizations as dynamic transformation systems

A transformation system is defined as dynamic if the transformation evolves over time so as to produce a stream of outputs resulting from transformations implemented on a stream of inputs. We call a system's trajectory the dynamics taken on by the inputs and outputs that are considered significant to observe over time. We have considered the nonprofit organization as an institution created to last over time, and therefore over time it develops the inputs acquisition flows, the productive transformation flows, and the transfers of the products obtained; over time it obtains financing and capital; and over time it scales the invested capital according to the needs of production and recipients. The nonprofit firm can thus be considered a temporally dynamic transformation system. The trajectory of the system is defined by the dynamics of its values over time and more specifically in the different administrative periods in which management is partitioned.

Notes

1 The reference framework is Mella's systemic theory (Mella, 2022, 2021a, 2021b, 2017, 2014, 2012a, 2008, 1992, 1997; Mella & Gazzola, 2019; Mella & Rangone, 2019).
2 Utility is the aptitude of goods to satisfy needs or enable the attainment of desires.
3 Productivity can be defined as the ratio between product quantity and quality, and a corresponding volume of inputs employed to obtain it (Tessitore, 1979).
4 The world is shifting from an ethics and aesthetics that reflect the uncritical acceptance of unlimited growth to an ethics and aesthetics that reflect the less-than-functional consequences of unlimited growth. The new model to follow is one of quality and development. Mitroff (1988) states that in this case "Less often leads to more".
5 The invested capital taken into consideration is Net Invested Capital given by the algebraic sum of:

+ working capital
− short-term liabilities
+ net fixed assets

References

Airoldi, G. (1996). *Le aziende nonprofit: Definizioni e classificazioni, within Le aziende non profit tra stato e mercato.* Bologna: Clueb.

Amaduzzi, A. (1967). *L'azienda: nel suo sistema e nell'ordine delle sue rilevazioni.* Torino: Utet.

Ashby, W. R. (1964). *An introduction to Cybernetics.* London: Chaplan & Hall.

Bertini, U. (1988). *Il sistema d'azienda.* Torino: Giappichelli.

Borgonovi, E. (1996). *Aziende non profit: problemi teorici, profili giuridici e politiche di indirizzo.* Bologna: Clueb.

Canziani, A. (2007). Economia Aziendale and Betriebswirtschaftslehre as autonomous sciences of the firm. *The firm as an entity and its economy.* London: Routledge, 107–130.

Capaldo, P. (1996). *Le aziende non profit: definizioni e classificazioni. Aa. Vv., Le aziende non profit tra stato e mercato.* Bologna: Atti del convegno Aidea, Clueb.

Coda, V. (1988). *L'orientamento strategico dell'impresa.* Torino: Utet.

Contrafatto, M., & Rusconi, G. (2005). Social accounting in Italy: Origins and developments. *Social and Environmental Accountability Journal, 25*(2), 3–8.

Coronella, S., Caputo, F., Leopizzi, R., & Venturelli, A. (2018). Corporate social responsibility in Economia Aziendale scholars' theories: A taxonomic perspective. *Meditari Accountancy Research, 26*(4), 640–656.

Ferrero, G. (1987). *Impresa e management.* Milano: Giuffrè.

Galassi, G., & Mattessich, R. (2004). Italian accounting research in the first half of the 20th century. *Review of Accounting and Finance, 3*(2), 62–83.

Gazzola, P., & Mella, P. (2012). Corporate performance and corporate social responsibility (CSR). *A Necessary Choice?. Economia Aziendale Online, 3*(3), 1–22.

Mella, P. (1979). *L'azienda di produzione quale trasformatore economico.* Pavia: Gjes.

Mella, P. (1992). *Economia Aziendale.* Torino: Utet.

Mella, P. (1997). *Dai Sistemi al pensiero sistemico: per capire i sistemi e pensare con i sistemi* (Vol. 28). Milano: FrancoAngeli.

Mella P. (2008). Systems thinking e system dynamics. l'arte di capire la dinamica ed il controllo dei sistemi. *Economia Aziendale 2000 Web (ISSN:1826-4719), 4/2008,* 153–192.

Mella, P. (2012a). *Systems thinking. Intelligence in action.* New York, Dordrecht, London: Springer.

Mella, P. (2012b). Performance indicators in business value-creating organizations. *Economia Aziendale Online, 2*(2), 25–52.

Mella, P. (2014). *Teoria del controllo. Dal Systems Thinking ai Sistemi di Controllo.* (pp. 1–408). Milano: Franco Angeli.

Mella, P. (2017). The unexpected cybernetics life of collectivities. The combinatory systems approach. *Kybernetes, 46*(7), 1086–1111.

Mella, P. (2021a, 1st Ed. 2014). *The magic ring. Systems thinking approach to control systems* (Second Edition). Switzerland: Springer Nature.

Mella, P. (2021b). Entrepreneurial dynamics and clusters formation. *The Combinatory Systems View. Economia Aziendale Online, 12*(1), 99–124.

Mella, P. (2022). Global warming: Is It (im)possible to stop it? The systems thinking approach. *Energies, 15*(705), 1–33.

Mella P., & Gazzola P. (2019). Improving managers' intelligence through systems thinking. *Kybernetes, 48*(1), 58–78.

Mella, P., & Rangone A. (2019). Obstacles to managing dynamic systems. The systems thinking approach. *International Journal of Business and Social Science, 10*(8), 24–41.

Mitroff, I. I. (1988). Business not as usual, rethinking our individual, corporate, and industrial strategies for global competition. *Journal of Business Ethics, 7*(9), 723–724.

Paolone, G., & D'Amico, L. (1994). *L'economia aziendale nei suoi principi parametrici e modelli applicativi.* Torino: Giappichelli.

Rusconi, G. (2019). Ethical firm system and stakeholder management theories: A possible convergence. *European Management Review, 16*(1), 147–166.

Signori, S., & Rusconi, G. (2009). Ethical thinking in traditional Italian Economia Aziendale and the stakeholder management theory: The search for possible interactions. *Journal of Business Ethics, 89*(3), 303–318.

Superti Furga, F. (1971). *Osservazioni sulla logica operativa dei sistemi aziendali integrati.* Milano: Giuffrè.

Tessitore, A. (1979). *Redditività dell'impresa in periodi di inflazione.* Cedam.

Tessitore, A. (1996). *La produzione e la distribuzione del valore. Le aziende non profit tra Stato e Mercato.* CLUEB.

Zappa, G. (1937). *Il reddito d'impresa.* Milano: Giuffrè.

Zappa, G. (1956). *Le produzioni nell'economia delle imprese: tomo primo.* Milano: Giuffrè.

3 Identifying and Determining the Relevant Dimensions for Performance Measurement

3.1 The concept of performance measurement in the organization

To address the problem of determining performance dimensions, it is necessary to analyze:

- the concept of measurement in general (Bandalos, 2018), specifying the meanings and content that can be attributed to the measurement activity;
- the concept of performance measurement of an organization in general (Asiaei & Bontis, 2019; Owais & Kiss, 2020; Pattanasak et al., 2022);
- the specific features of performance measurement in nonprofit organizations (Anheier & Leat, 2018; Lee, 2021; Treinta et al., 2020).

Performance is a complex concept that in this chapter is used to highlight, from a quantitative and qualitative perspective (Giannessi, 1979), the result or set of results achieved by an organization when carrying out its activities (Comuzzi, 1996). In other words, the suggestion is to measure achievement outcomes related to organizational and management choices and actions (Zappa, 1927). A well-known saying states, "You get what you measure and reward" (Ezzamel, 1996), this means that measurement, and especially the measurement of organizations, has not only the task of depicting observed phenomena, but also that of playing a fundamental role in supporting coordinated actions by guiding decision-making processes (Drucker, 1973; Mason & Swanson, 1981). To define it, measurements can be compared to a magnifying glass that can be used to observe the organizational reality (Garengo & Bernardi, 2007; Garengo, Biazzo & Bititci, 2005; Martini & Suardana, 2019): like any lens, it can magnify, reduce, distort, or alter the observed images

DOI: 10.4324/9781003350439-4

(Mason & Swanson, 1988). The measurement problem leads to the definition of the reality to be observed and the identification of the measurement system (Edwards, 1986) best suited to guide organizational and managerial behavior (Silvi, 1995). Measurement can be configured as a system of methodologies, structures, and processes that detect expected or achieved performance results to communicate, interpret, guide, and evaluate organizational behaviors preordained to achieve objectives. The measure must be chosen according to the specificity and needs of the users (Amaduzzi, 1967; Giannessi, 1979; Onida, 1951). It has the function of highlighting problems relevant to the management and of indicating the best courses of action to achieve the objectives (Brunetti, 1989). Therefore, it should be instrumental in the pursuit of business goals (Cooper & Kaplan, 1991; Johnson & Kaplan, 1987). The system of measures must be assessed in relation to the specificity of the company and the effects it will have on the company's overall performance (Airoldi, 1989). The tasks of business performance measurement can be summarized as follows:

• to enable the interpretation of the dynamics of business phenomena relevant to the achievement of objectives;
• to guide and stimulate behavior consistent with the goals (Anthony, Dearden, & Bedford, 1989) to be achieved (Amigoni, 1979).

It is important for the measures adopted to be simple so as to facilitate the establishment of outcome standards that can guide the judgment regarding performance (Ezzamel, 1996). In organizations, acting as finalized systems, performance consists of the measure of the degree to which the predetermined goals of cost-effectiveness are achieved in terms of efficiency and effectiveness (Cassandro, 1979; Giannessi, 1961; Zangrandi, 1994). The notion of performance recalls the concepts of "cost-effectiveness" (Campra et al, 2021), understood as the ability over time to adequately remunerate the factors of production employed (D'Amico, 2008), and of "value creation" (Freudenreich, Lüdeke-Freund & Schaltegger, 2020; Guatri, 1991), expressions used to convey the ability of companies to pursue over time the goals for which they were established. In order to examine the conditions for the existence of organizations over time, it is necessary to analyze the organization's aptitude for durability (Zappa, 1956). This aptitude is related to two other fundamental characteristics: economic independence (Onida, 1989) and continuity (Marcon, 1984). The pursuit of the principle of cost-effectiveness, especially with reference to the mid- to long-term, allows the fulfillment of the characteristics of durability, independence, and continuity. Thanks to the adequate remuneration of all the factors of production employed, the expectations of the various business stakeholders are met (Coda, 1991) and the foundations are laid for the consolidation and development of the organization itself (Bertini, 1992). In the management of economic value, it is evident the task of managerial and entrepreneurial skills in knowing how to integrate the different contributions leading them to effective value creation (Bruni, 1994). Business performance represents the yardstick for measuring and evaluating the contributions of the plurality of production factors, resources, organizational entities, and business stakeholders and their ability. In other words, it constitutes the yardstick for measuring and evaluating the results of corporate performance, economic coordination, strategic, organizational and managerial profiles (Coda, 1988).

3.2 The appreciation of a transformation system

The analysis of transformation systems implies the possibility of implementing appreciations. We indicate with the term "appreciation" the possibility of having meaningful indicators of the transformation implemented within a given system and, moreover, the possibility of comparing it with similar indicators determined for systems used as benchmarks. To implement appreciation, it is necessary to seek the dimensions that characterize the essential aspects of the transformation dynamics carried out within the system. The fundamental dimensions of analysis of a positive transformation dynamic system are:

- efficiency;
- effectiveness;
- yield.

We can define the efficiency of a processing system as the ability to produce a convenient gap between input and output measures[1] (Guatri, 1950). Depending on the gap, some degree of efficiency is achieved. Efficiency, according to a generally accepted definition, can be quantified as the ratio of output to input (Barnard, 1968), that is, the amount of output per unit of input (Horngren, 1987):

$$\text{efficiency} = \frac{\text{actual outputs}}{\text{actual inputs}}$$

The transformation system normally tends to seek the optimum, so we can consider efficiency as the system's tendency to seek the maximum gap between input and output. More precisely:

• to maximize outputs given the same amount of inputs;
• to minimize inputs given the same amount of outputs.

The effectiveness of a processing system represents the system's ability to conveniently achieve given goals expressed in terms of outputs. The greater a system's ability to achieve goals, the greater its effectiveness. Effectiveness can be expressed as the ratio of outputs to goals:

$$effectiveness = \frac{output}{goals}$$

In order to analyze effectiveness, the following comparisons can be made:

• the outputs of the system and the outputs of a reference system;
• the actual outputs with the planned outputs;
• the actual outputs with the outputs that needed to be given up in order to carry out the transformation.

In nonprofit organizations it can also be interpreted as the ratio between satisfaction achieved and expected levels of satisfaction:

$$effectiveness = \frac{extent \ of \ satisfaction \ obtained}{expected \ levels \ of \ satisfaction (goals)}$$

Transformation yield represents the ability to obtain higher results in relation to the resources employed. Yield can be expressed as the ratio of results to resources employed:

$$yield = \frac{output - input}{resources \ employed} = \frac{results}{resources \ employed}$$

3.3 The appreciation of the nonprofit organization transformation system

From what was learned in the previous paragraphs, the organization seen as a system of productive, economic, and financial transformations, appears to be characterized by three forms of efficiency (Mella, 1992):

- productive efficiency;
- economic efficiency;
- financial efficiency.

The organization viewed as a system of managerial transformation is characterized by effectiveness, that is, the ability to achieve the goals underlying managerial transformation. The achievement of goals represents the fundamental element of existence of the nonprofit organization. Every decision (Figure 3.1), an output of managerial transformation aimed at achieving goals, must necessarily consider the levels of efficiency produced by that decision within the productive, economic, and financial transformations implemented by the operations adopted.

3.4 Performance in nonprofit organizations

The performance is designed to provide a measure of the degree of goal accomplishment, both those freely chosen and those imposed by the system-environment which the company is a part of (Guatri, 1997), in terms of effectiveness and efficiency, and thus the degree to which the expectations of monetary and nonmonetary value of the resources provided by the various corporate parties, also referred to as stakeholders (Carroll, 1989; Clarkson, 1991; Donaldson & Preston, 1995; Freeman, 1984; Hill & Jones, 1992) are met. Thus, the basis for a lasting strengthening and development of the organization is created (Coda, 1991) as well as collective economic utility. In these organizations, maximization of residual economic value, i.e., profit as an economic category, is not a guiding criterion, nor is it a parameter that can be used to assess the degree of success and to make judgments about the degree of technical, organizational, and economic rationality employed in carrying out activities (Borgonovi, 1996). Therefore, the concept of cost-effectiveness is used by attributing to it a broad content (Catturi, 1994), which basically coincides with the conditions for the survival and development of the company (Zangrandi, 1996). Cost-effectiveness concerns the company as a whole in a medium- to long-term time perspective, toward whose consolidation or development contributes a plurality of production factors, resources, organizational entities, and stakeholders. In nonprofit organizations, performance indicators should refer to the following elements:

- physical-technical such as, for example, volumes and quality of services;

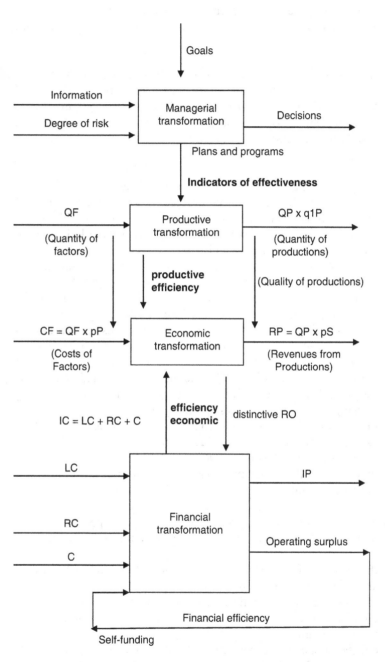

Figure 3.1 The nonprofit organization model as a transformational system and the indicators for appreciation.

- monetary such as costs, revenues, surpluses, and deficits;
- ethical and moral such as whether or not they are consistent with certain values.

The latter is the biggest problem to be addressed because, in the absence of a valid measurement system, there is a risk of ideological contrasts prevailing over business results. The measure system must be evaluated in relation to the specificity of nonprofit organizations that have the following characteristics (Molteni, 1997):

- have a private nature, thus stemming from the initiative of private individuals and are aimed at the achievement of the purposes established by them, operating in freedom and autonomy; even if they do not set as their operational rationale that of exchange in order to obtain a profit (Capaldo, 1996) they are not linked to the State(Airoldi, 1996; Ponzanelli, 1985);
- the origin, evolution, and operation of these organizations are driven by a profound ideological rationale (Zamagni, 1997); even the choice of individuals working in such organizations is backed by ideological motives such as sharing corporate purpose, altruism, and so on, all of which obviously conditions organizational variables that take on distinctive traits compared to businesses (Pezzani, 1998);
- their existence is legitimized by the quantity and quality of needs satisfied; hence production is not instrumental in increasing exchange value, but it represents the goal;
- they are aimed at producing goods or services to meet the needs of users', hence they are producers (or destroyers) of wealth (Capaldo, 1996; Tessitore, 1996);
- they may not distribute any operating surplus, but must reinvest it in the organization.

If we consider nonprofit organizations from the perspective of organizational variables, we can highlight the following peculiarities:

- they possess strong business motivation, a low level of hierarchy, and a high sense of cooperation;
- in achieving goals, attention is paid not only to efficiency and cost-effectiveness, but also to cooperation between individuals working in the company;
- efforts are made to generate social utility and to keep the level of interpersonal conflicts to a minimum;

- there is an automatic allocation of responsibilities and a pursuit of them therefore no complex organizational mechanisms are required;
- staff are also chosen on the basis of individuals' ideal motivations;
- the social and human values of these companies contribute to raising awareness within the community (Pezzani, 1998).

In evaluating the performance of nonprofit organizations, it is worth considering that any business in which goods and services are manufactured can be a wealth generator. This depends on the relationship between the values produced and the values consumed (economic transformation) to obtain these productions. If the economic transformation reveals that the values produced are greater than the values consumed the organization has generated wealth, whatever form it takes and whoever benefits from it. The challenge lies in quantifying the input and output values of the economic transformation, so it is difficult to quantify the wealth generated (Capaldo, 1996). Even nonprofit organizations must apply the principles, criteria, methods, and techniques of managerial, organizational, and economic efficiency because there is no logical, philosophical, or moral reason for a trade-off between motivation and economic rationality.

3.5 The performance determinants

Performance has been defined as the result, or rather the accomplishments resulting from the execution of organizational and managerial processes. It is aimed at the management and improvement of efficiency and effectiveness performance, which in turn can be defined through different criteria. These organizations have special characteristics that give rise to performance measurement issues:

- the goods and services offered (Arcari, 1991; Heskett et al., 1994) are often characterized by a high degree of intangibility, thus it is difficult to assess the quality of goods and services because it often depends on the ability to create an atmosphere of trust and cordiality (Mosca, 1994; Newman & Wallender 1978; Thompson & McEwen, 1958);
- often not a single good or service is offered, but rather a set of activities;
- there is often a contemporaneity between production and consumption, in these cases it is difficult to store the output of the productive transformation;

- the output of the production process, in most cases, is customized according to the individual needs of users (Santesso & Sostero, 1987);
- the goods and services considered have the goal of increasing the well-being of the person (Drucker, 1990);
- it is difficult for users to evaluate the quality of the goods or services because they normally do not rely only on the result, but are influenced by the process (Zeithaml et al., 1990).

The problem with performance measurement can be analyzed from two perspectives:

1   from an internal point of view, as the organization's ability to develop autopoietic behavior by continuously reintegrating the network of internal processes that characterizes it;
2   from an external point of view, considering instead the nonprofit organization in its manifestations of existence and thus in terms of its ability to survive in the environment in which it carries out its institutional activities.

Internal performance indications are meant to bring out the conditions of endogenous teleonomy, while external performance indications are meant to bring out these organizations' conditions of exogenous teleonomy. Efficiency and effectiveness performance are linked by a two-way relationship in that the degree of endogenous teleonomy influences exogenous teleonomy and vice versa (Figure 3.2).

Performance management and improvement area

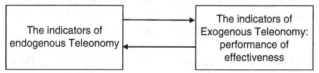

Figure 3.2 Overview of the measurement system.

Taken, with adaptations, from Silvi, R. (1995). La progettazione del sistema di misurazione della performance aziendale. Giappichelli, Torino, p. 45.

The accomplishments that determine the company's performance are not necessarily representable or detectable with monetary parameters; they must be measured through quantitative and qualitative parameters that express the phenomenon. The more the measure expresses and represents the phenomenon, the greater will be the opportunities for performance improvement. Accounting data (Johnson, 1994), being results and not causes of performance, could only indirectly and partially detect the determinants of performance.[2]

3.6 The measurement system

The plurality of performance, and related measures, and the high degree of integration and interdependence, make the design of a measurement system complex. It must relate to the specific business reality, the objectives to be achieved, and the needs and characteristics of users (Cassandro, 1985). It is not possible to formulate universally valid solutions because measurement may prove ineffective. The system of performance measures is peculiar to each individual organization therefore specific categories of indicators having normative character will not be presented. The proposed system is intended to emphasize an analysis of a global nature aimed at measuring the results of the organization's system seen in its complexity and an analysis of an analytical nature relating to the development of suitable parameters to represent the result of the specific actions put in place to achieve the organization's goals. In real-life situations, effectiveness and efficiency appear as linked and intertwined, and many indicators contain information on both one and the other dimension. Figure 3.3 shows the connection and interrelationships between the indicators of effectiveness and efficiency derived from the model of the nonprofit organization, considered as a system of four transformers. First of all, the effectiveness of the operations of nonprofit organizations is measured in terms of the satisfaction of customer/user expectations. However, the degree of satisfaction can be influenced by the price paid, the latter in turn being related to unit cost and thus efficiency. Fulfillment of the expectations of the promoter, of the staff, is mainly evaluated with indicators of effectiveness, but is still influenced by efficiency. For the evaluation of the fulfillment of the expectations of donors who wish to see money invested in activities that show results, the indicators will be efficiency and effectiveness. Productive efficiency represents the typical efficiency indicator, expressed through yields. These are indicators that refer to physical quantities in output and input.[3] Economic efficiency in nonprofit organizations should not be considered only by taking into account break-even in accounting terms, but should be interpreted in a broad sense as the increase and enhancement of resource assets and as the preservation over time of conditions that meet and guarantee the expectations of stakeholders. Therefore, it is an indicator of efficiency

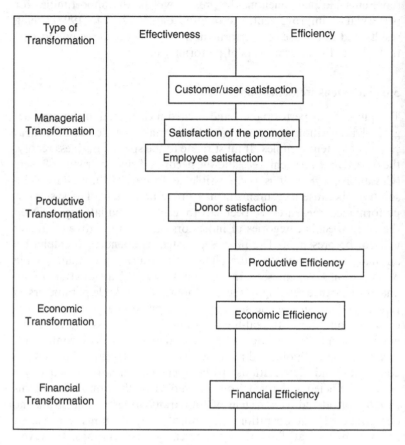

Figure 3.3 The efficiency and effectiveness indicators of the organization as a system of four transformations.

that is, however, influenced by effectiveness. Financial efficiency should be interpreted as the ability of the organization to achieve a financial fueling mechanism for development, including qualitative development, through the production of operating surpluses that can be reinvested in the business.

3.7 The characteristics of an optimal performance indicator system

A system of indicators should be designed bearing in mind that the organizational performance indicators that are used should be the ones that are really effective (Riccaboni, 1989). It is therefore necessary to take into account the following requirements:

- the individual indicators must be good predictors of a dimension of organizational performance;
- the system of indicators (Farneti, Mazzara & Savioli, 1996; Zangrandi, 1985) must enable organizational performance to be captured both in the relevant individual dimensions and as a whole.

Individual indicators should possess the following characteristics:

- consistency with the organization's goals;
- accuracy;
- reliability;
- objectivity;
- comparability;
- flexibility.

First of all, an indicator, in order for it to be considered a valid indicator, should reflect the real goals of the organization. Some indicators directly express the organization's performance, others may be connected to it with a more or less long causal chain. Especially when we use surrogate indicators of certain phenomena, it is necessary to remember the simplifying assumptions underlying the adoption of such measures (Anthony & Young, 1988). Secondly, indicators should be precise by referencing the accuracy with which a certain dimension is determined. A high degree of accuracy is achieved if, using multiple mutually independent measures, the dispersion that is identified among the values that can be obtained for a certain area of results is minimal (Riccaboni, 1989). Reliability indicates the ability of an indicator to produce the same results in repeated determinations made under the same conditions, taking into account possible observational errors (Delvecchio, 1995). The characteristic of objectivity indicates that any personal opinions or influences exercised by the performance evaluator should be absent. Of course, in the case where the measurement activity and the evaluation of results are carried out by the same person, objectivity will be low. To overcome this problem it's advisable to:

- assign the task of conducting measurements to people not directly involved in the evaluation process;
- assign the task of verification to independent operators whenever possible.

Comparability highlights the informational significance of an indicator. The latter will be greater the higher the possibility of comparison with values observed at other organizations. Of course, it is necessary for other companies to adopt the same type of indicators and for the basic data used in the construction of the indicators to be homogeneous. Flexibility shows the ability of an indicator to balance a sufficient degree of generality, to allow its application in the different economic-market sectors in which nonprofit organizations operate, with a high degree of specificity, to be able to propose results that are not already known. Regarding the conditions for the use of indicators, it is necessary to consider:

- timeliness;
- understandability (Merchant, 1985);
- detectability.

Timeliness is a characteristic to be considered for two reasons:

- if measurement is not conducted in a timely manner, it is impossible to take action to prevent the problems that the performance indicators foreshadow;
- recognition of inefficiency or good performance, if it is not available on time, it loses most of its motivational effect (Riccaboni, 1989).

Performance indicators can also achieve the goal of motivating people, but this can occur when people are able to understand the meaning of the indicator used and how to improve it (Merchant, 1985). Detectability pertains to the possibility of detecting data through observation of business reality. In fact, some information may not have been recorded at the appropriate time or operators may not have known the techniques for doing so. If the indicator under investigation is characterized by all the qualities just described, it can be argued that it can form the basis for an evaluation activity and for carrying out a proper monitoring of the results. If not, it will be necessary to assess the validity of individual outcome measures and make a trade-off between the listed criteria.

The requisites that a good indicator system must possess are the general design criteria, we point out:

- comprehensiveness;
- selectivity;
- convenience (Molteni, 1997).

Comprehensiveness concerns the ability to consider all relevant dimensions in order to reach an assessment of the phenomenon under consideration. Selectivity is related to the need not to use an overly broad system of parameters that result in excessive costs and time, and that divert attention from important information. Convenience leads to cost-benefit analysis. The benefits that result from data collection in terms of knowledge about the object of investigation must outweigh the costs involved, both in terms of time and the expense associated with its use. The interpretation of an indicator should not only be considered on its own, but it is often necessary to analyze it together with other measures concerning the same phenomenon.

Notes

1 Production efficiency indicators are called yields.
2 The accounting-monetary measure is a tool, even if indirect or mediated, to guide toward conditions of efficiency, effectiveness, and cost-effectiveness.
3 Productivity indicators in nonprofit organizations were discussed, among others, by Hayes & Millar, 1990; Davis, 1991; Mensah & Li, 1993.

References

Airoldi, G. (1989). *L'organizzazione. Airoldi G., Brunetti G. e Coda V., Lezioni di Economia Aziendale*. Bologna: Il Mulino.

Airoldi, G. (1996). *Le aziende nonprofit: definizioni e classificazioni. Atti del Convegno dell'Accademia Italiana di Economia Aziendale"*. Bologna: Clueb.

Amaduzzi, A. (1967). *L'azienda: nel suo sistema e nell'ordine delle sue rilevazioni*. Torino: Utet.

Amigoni, F. (1979). *I sistemi di controllo direzionale: criteri di progettazione e di impiego*. Milano: Giuffrè.

Anheier, H. K., & Leat, D. (2018). *Performance measurement in Philanthropic foundations: The ambiguity of success and failure*. Routledge.

Anthony, R. N., & Young, D. W. (1988). *Management control in non-profit organizations*. Illinois: IRWIN, Homewood.

Anthony, R. N., Dearden, J., & Bedford, N. M. (1989). *Management control systems*. Illinois: Irwin, Homewood.

Arcari, A. M. (1991). *Economia delle imprese di servizi professionali: logiche e strumenti di controllo*. Bocconi: EGEA, Ed. Giuridiche Economiche Aziendali dell'Univ.

Asiaei, K., & Bontis, N. (2019). Translating knowledge management into performance: The role of performance measurement systems. *Management Research Review*, *43*(1), 113–132.

Bandalos, D. L. (2018). *Measurement theory and applications for the social sciences*. New York: Guilford Publications.

Barnard, C. I. (1968). *The functions of the executive* (Vol. 11). Cambridge, Massachusetts: Harvard University Press.

Bertini, U. (1992). Fattori di successo e condizioni di sviluppo delle piccole e medie imprese. *Studi e informazioni, 1*(1), 1–53.

Borgonovi, E. (1996). *Aziende non profit: problemi teorici, profili giuridici e politiche di indirizzo.* Bologna: Clueb.

Brunetti, G. (1989). L'economicità e la rilevazione. In G. Airoldi, G. Brunetti, V. Coda (Eds.), *Lezioni di Economia aziendale* (pp. 112-160). Bologna: Il Mulino.

Bruni, G. (1994). *Analisi del valore: il contributo dell' "Activity based management".* Torino: Giappichelli.

Campra, M., Paola, O., Stefano, A., & Brescia, V. (2021). Ordering cost-effectiveness management studies in healthcare: A PRISMA-Compliant systematic literature review and bibliometric analysis. *International Journal of Business Administration, 12*(4), 45–68.

Capaldo, P. (1996). *Le aziende non profit: definizioni e classificazioni. Aa. Vv., Le aziende non profit tra stato e mercato.* Bologna: Atti del convegno Aidea, Clueb.

Carroll, A. B. (1989). *Business and society: Ethics and stakeholder management.* Cincinnati, OH: South-Western.

Cassandro, P. E. (1979). *Le gestioni erogatrici pubbliche.* Torino: Utet.

Cassandro, P. E. (1985). Sulla cosiddetta performance dell'azienda e sulla possibilità di una sua valutazione. *Rivista Italiana di Ragioneria,* 4–5.

Catturi, G. (1994). *La teoria dei flussi e degli stocks ed il" sistema dei valori" d'impresa: conversazioni con gli studenti sulla" creazione del valore".* Milano: Cedam.

Clarkson, M. B. (1991). Defining, evaluating, and managing corporate social performance: The stakeholder management model. *Research in Corporate Social Performance and Policy, 12*(1), 331–358.

Coda, V. (1988). *L'orientamento strategico dell'impresa.* Torino: Utet.

Coda, V. (1991). Il problema della valutazione della strategia. *Economia e Management,* n. 12, p. 91.

Comuzzi, E. (1996). *La misurazione della performance nelle aggregazioni aziendali.* Padova: CEDAM.

Cooper, R., & Kaplan, R. S. (1991). *The design of cost management systems: Text, cases, and readings.* Englewood Cliffs, N.J: Prentice Hall.

D'Amico, L. (2008). L'evoluzione degli studi sull'economia dell'azienda: Brevi considerazioni sull'inquadramento della disciplina. In G. Paolone & L. D'Amico (Ed.), *L'economia aziendale nei suoi principi parametrici e modelli applicativi.* Torino: Giappichelli.

Davis, T. R. (1991). Internal service operations: Strategies for increasing their effectiveness and controlling their cost. *Organizational Dynamics, 20*(2), 5–22.

Delvecchio, F. (1995). *Scale di misura e indicatori sociali.* Bari: Cacucci.

Donaldson, T., & Preston, L. E. (1995). The stakeholder theory of the corporation: Concepts, evidence, and implications. *Academy of Management Review, 20*(1), 65–91.

Drucker, P. (1973). *Management: Tasks, responsibilities, practices Harper &* *Row*. New York: Publishers.

Drucker, P. F. (1990). Lessons for successful nonprofit governance. *Nonprofit Management and Leadership, 1*(1), 7–14.

Edwards, J. B. (1986). *The use of performance measures*. Montvale, New Jersey: National Association of Accountants.

Ezzamel, M. (1996). *La misurazione e la valutazione della performance divisionale: parametri contabili, finanziari e qualitativi*. EGEA.

Farneti, G., Mazzara, L., & Savioli, G. (1996). *Il sistema degli indicatori negli enti locali*. Torino: Giappichelli.

Freudenreich, B., Lüdeke-Freund, F., & Schaltegger, S. (2020). A stakeholder theory perspective on business models: Value creation for sustainability. *Journal of Business Ethics, 166*(1), 3–18.

Freeman, R. E. (1984). *Strategic management: A stakeholder approach*. Boston: Pitman Pub_Lishing.

Garengo, P., Biazzo, S., & Bititci, U. S. (2005). Performance measurement systems in SMEs: A review for a research agenda. *International Journal of Management Reviews, 7*(1), 25–47.

Garengo, P., & Bernardi, G. (2007). Organizational capability in SMEs: Performance measurement as a key system in supporting company development. *International Journal of Productivity and Performance Management, 56*(5/6), pp. 518–532.

Giannessi, E. (1961). *Interpretazione del concetto di azienda pubblica*. Pisa: Cursi.

Giannessi, E. (1979). *Appunti di economia aziendale*. Pisa: Pacini.

Guatri, L. (1950). *I rendimenti*. Giuffrè.

Guatri, L. (1991). *La teoria di creazione del valore: una via europea*. Milano: Egea.

Guatri, L. (1997). *Valore e intangibles nella misura della performance aziendale: un percorso storico* (p. 218). Milano: Egea.

Hayes, R. D., & Millar, J. A. (1990). Measuring production efficiency in a not-for-profit setting. *Accounting Review, 65*(3), 505–519.

Heskett, J. L., Jones, T. O., Loveman, G. W., Sasser, W. E., & Schlesinger, L. A. (1994). Putting the service-profit chain to work. *Harvard Business Review, 72*(2), 164–174.

Hill, C. W., & Jones, T. M. (1992). Stakeholder-agency theory. *Journal of Management Studies, 29*(2), 131–154.

Horngren, C. T. (1987). *Cost accounting: A management emphasis*. Englewood Cliffs, New Jersey: Prentice Hall, International.

Johnson, T. H., & Kaplan, R. S. (1987). *Relevance lost: The rise and fall of management accounting*. Cambridge, MA: Harvard Business School Press.

Johnson, H. T. (1994). Relevance regained: Total quality management and the role of management accounting. *Critical Perspectives on Accounting, 5*(3), 259–267.

Lee, C. (2021). Factors influencing the credibility of performance measurement in nonprofits. *International Review of Public Administration, 26*(2), 156–174.

Marcon, G. (1984). *Le imprese a partecipazione pubblica: Finalitá pubbliche ed economicità*. Milani, Padova: CEDAM-Casa Ed.

Martini, L. K. B., & Suardana, I. B. R. (2019). Company performance measurement applying balanced scorecard approach. *International Journal of Social Sciences and Humanities*, 3(1), 7–13.

Mason, R. O., & Swanson, E. B. (1981). *Measurement for management decision*. Addison Wesley Publishing Company.

Mason, R. O., & Swanson, E. B. (1988). *Gli indici di valutazione per le decisioni aziendali*. Amigoni F. (a cura di), Misurazioni d'azienda, Giuffré, Milano.

Merchant, K. A. (1985). *Control in business organizations*. Cambridge, Massachusetts: Harpercollins College Division. Ballinger Publishing Company.

Mella, P. (1992). *Economia Aziendale*. Torino: Utet.

Mensah, Y. M., & Li, S. H. (1993). Measuring production efficiency in a not-for-profit setting: An extension. *Accounting Review*, 68(1), 66–88.

Molteni, M. M. (1997). *Le misure di performance nelle aziende non profit di servizio alla persona*. Padova: Cedam.

Mosca, F. (1994). *Aspetti strategici della qualità totale nei servizi*. Giappichelli, Torino.

Newman, W. H., & Wallender III, H. W. (1978). Managing not-for-profit enterprises. *Academy of Management Review*, 3(1), 24–31.

Onida, P. (1951). *Le discipline economico-aziendali: Oggetto e metodo*. Giuffrè.

Onida, P. (1989). *Economia d'azienda*. Torino: Utet.

Owais, L., & Kiss, J. T. (2020). The effects of using performance measurement systems (PMSS) on organization performance. *Cross-Cultural Management Journal*, 22(2), 111–121.

Pattanasak, P., Anantana, T., Paphawasit, B., & Wudhikarn, R. (2022). Critical factors and performance measurement of business incubators: A systematic literature review. *Sustainability*, 14(8), 4610.

Pezzani, F. (1998). Le aziende non profit ed il contributo delle scienze economico-aziendali. Il ruolo delle determinazioni quantitative contabili. G. Concari (a cura di), "Enti non profit", Summit, Supplemento al, (27).

Ponzanelli, G. (1985). *Le "non profit organizations"* (Vol. 69). Giuffrè.

Riccaboni, A. (1989). *La misurazione della performance dei centri di profitto, critica agli strumenti tradizionali e nuovi orientamenti d'indagine*. Padova: Cedam.

Santesso, E., & Sostero, U. (1987). *Strumenti per il controllo di gestione nelle unità sanitarie locali*. CEDAM.

Silvi, R. (1995). *La progettazione del sistema di misurazione della performance aziendale*. Torino: Giappichelli.

Tessitore, A. (1996). *La produzione e la distribuzione del valore. Le aziende non profit tra Stato e Mercato*. Bologna: Clueb.

Thompson, J. D., & McEwen, W. J. (1958). Organizational goals and environment: Goal-setting as an interaction process. *American Sociological Review*, 23(1), 23–31.

Treinta, F. T., Moura, L. F., Almeida Prado Cestari, J. M., Pinheiro de Lima, E., Deschamps, F., Gouvea da Costa, S. E., ... & Leite, L. R. (2020). Design and implementation factors for performance measurement in non-profit organizations: A literature review. *Frontiers in Psychology, 11*, 1799.

Zamagni, S. (1997). *Il non profit della società postfordista alla ricerca di una nuova identità.* G. VITTADINI (a cura), Il non profit dimezzato, Etaslibri, Milano.

Zangrandi, A. (1985). *Il controllo di gestione nelle unità sanitarie locali.* Giuffrè.

Zangrandi, A. (1994). *Autonomia ed economicità nelle aziende pubbliche.* Giuffrè.

Zangrandi, A. (1996). Uno schema di classificazione delle organizzazioni nonprofit. AA. VV.(a cura di Borzaga, C., Fiorentini, G., & Matacena, A.), "Non profit e sistemi di Welfare, il contributo dell'analisi economica", La Nuova Italia Scientifica, Firenze.

Zappa, G. (1927). *Tendenze nuove negli studi di ragioneria: discorso inaugurale dell'anno accademico 1926-27 nel R. Istituto superiore di scienze economiche e commerciali di Venezia.* SA Istituto editoriale scientifico.

Zappa, G. (1956). *Le produzioni nell'economia delle imprese: Tomo primo.* Giuffrè, Milano.

Zeithaml, V. A., Parasuraman, A., Berry, L. L., & Berry, L. L. (1990). *Delivering quality service: Balancing customer perceptions and expectations.* New York: Simon and Schuster. The Free Press.

4 Internal Performance Indicators: The Endogenous Teleonomy

4.1 The lack of a synthesis indicator

In companies, the cost-revenue correlation is synthesized in the profit (Gholamhossein, Ali & Safdar, 2012; Mehar, 2005), and the operational logic of maximum efficiency leads to management tending toward maximum cost compression and maximum revenue expansion. Thus, enterprises have a well-defined and concrete performance indicator: the operating profit. In businesses, profit is the concise measure of business performance capable of reporting the existence of the indefinite living conditions of the business, the achievement of its goals and compliance with the efficiency standards by making rational use of available resources (Capaldo, 1996). In nonprofit organizations the outcomes to look at are not the same (McConville & Cordery, 2021; Nunamaker, 1985), in fact there is a general tendency to underestimate outcomes, believing that doing something to improve the lives of others is already an accomplishment. However, if a business squanders its resources on negative results, it loses its money; a nonprofit that produces nonresults loses the money of the individuals who have made contributions to the organization (Tarigan, 2012). Nonprofit companies are therefore accountable to donors for putting money into activities that demonstrate results and are responsible for the level of performance. Achieving and maintaining a self-sustaining financial and economic balance are the conditions for lasting functionality in nonprofit organizations as well; a prolonged imbalance would lead to the closure of the organization (Molteni, 1997). The peculiarity of nonprofit organizations does not allow the creation of a synthesis indicator endowed with the same reporting capacity that profit has in businesses. In these organizations it can only indicate the existence of balanced conditions of management, but it does not give an indication of the achievement of goals and the effectiveness and efficiency with

DOI: 10.4324/9781003350439-5

which the resources have been employed (Travaglini, 1992). A nonprofit organization may have a balanced financial report because it manages to keep expenses within the limits of income, however, it may have inefficiently carried out production, with a waste of resources, and it may also have failed to achieve its purposes (Kanter & Summers, 1994) and thus failed to pursue its productive mission. A positive income result can be influenced by several factors (Airoldi, Brunetti & Coda, 2020):

- purchase of production factors under particularly favorable conditions;
- special market conditions that allow any inefficiencies to be transferred externally;
- lower employee wages than those of businesses and unpaid labor;
- interruption of investment in training, research, development, etc., which create the conditions for the long-term life and development of the organization in the future.

The evaluation of cost-effectiveness in nonprofit organizations (Alves & Andersen, 2019) should not be carried out only by taking into account the break-even in accounting terms, but should be interpreted as increasing and enhancing the resource base and maintaining the conditions for meeting and guaranteeing the expectations of stakeholders over time. The organization must implement a financial feeding mechanism of qualitative development because the organization's functionality can only be sustained if continuous performance improvement is sought. Thus, economic analysis assumes fundamental relevance even in these nonprofit-oriented organizations because it enables the achievement of extra-economic ends. To allow the organization to develop, it is first necessary to avoid losses that would eventually affect their own resources endowment and possibly generate an operating surplus that should self-finance the increase in their own resources endowment. This value will not represent a profit, but, from an accounting standpoint, an allocation to a reserve aimed at replenishing and increasing the organization's functionality. In order to evaluate the efficiency of a nonprofit organization (Mohan, Gopalakrishnan & Mizzi, 2013; Rosko, Al-Amin & Tavakoli, 2020), as noted in the Section 3.7 we will analyze the three forms of efficiency that characterize the organization viewed as a system of productive, economic, and financial transformation (Mella, 1992, 1997, 2008, 2012a, 2014, 2017, 2021a, 2021b, 2022; Mella & Gazzola, 2019; Mella & Rangone, 2019):

- productive efficiency, as an indicator of productive transformation;
- economic efficiency, as an indicator of economic transformation;
- financial efficiency, as an indicator of financial transformation.

4.2 The principle of efficiency in man's activity

Men, both as individuals and as organizations, are future-oriented beings, operating predominantly to achieve goals. It can be said that the most relevant human and social activities are goal-oriented. We can define man as being "teleological", that is, primarily oriented toward the achievement of voluntarily set ends. It is possible to represent the goal-oriented activity of man, with the diagram in Figure 4.1.

The diagram depicted in the figure indicates that goal-oriented activity is carried out for the achievement of given goals from which we gain a certain degree of satisfaction. Each activity requires a given sacrifice and allows a certain benefit or outcome to be obtained. The efficiency indicator is given by the ratio, already considered in Section 3.6,

$$\text{efficiency} = \frac{\text{obtainable benefits}}{\text{sacrifices to be made}}$$

If we assume that man always acts rationally, human actions will be carried out according to the following principle. In carrying out his

Figure 4.1 Man's goal-oriented activities: a diagram.

goal-oriented activities, man seeks to maximize the efficiency ratios of his actions.

Man will therefore seek to:

* minimize the sacrifices required to obtain given benefits;
* maximize the benefits for the same sacrifice.

To increase efficiency, individuals come together in organizations, that is, multi-personal structures characterized by unity of purpose, co-operation among members, and specialization.

4.3 Productive efficiency

If we consider the organization as a productive processing system that transforms given inputs into quantities of outputs according to the scheme already analyzed (Figure 2.2). We can consider productive or technical efficiency defined as the ability of the system to maximize the ratio between the amount of outputs obtained and the amount of factors employed to obtain them. It is expressed as the average factor performance ratio (Mella, 2012b; Ponikvar, Tajnikar & Pušnik, 2009):

$$\text{REND(Yeld)} = \frac{\text{Quantity of output productions}}{\text{Quantity of input factors}}$$

The yield ratio measures the amount of output obtained from a unit of factor employed. The opposite of this ratio represents the factor employment rate:

$$\text{IMP(employment)} = \frac{\text{Quantity of input factors}}{\text{Quantity of output productions}}$$

The employment rate measures the amount of factor required to obtain one unit of production. Productive efficiency represents the ability to maximize returns while simultaneously minimizing factor employment rates. It can also be called internal efficiency or combination efficiency and expresses the "goodness" of the internal, productive efficiency of the company. In nonprofit organizations, it can also be interpreted as the ratio of benefits obtained to sacrifices made:

$$\text{efficiency} = \frac{\text{extent of benefits obtained}}{\text{extent of sacrifices made}}$$

Efficiency (Usai, 1990), therefore, represents the ability to make the most rational use of factors in order to obtain certain outputs (Molteni, 1997).

$$\text{efficiency} = \frac{\text{Output(T)}}{\text{Input(T)}}$$

Normally, efficiency is the management characteristic of:

- minimizing the use of resources and related costs for the same volumes achieved and their quality[1] in period T;
- maximizing volumes and qualities for the same amount of resources used and their costs in period T.

The main efficiency measures are given by the ratio between:

- the amount of resources used and the volume of activity obtained in carrying out the organization's processes;
- the amount of resources used and the results achieved by the activities carried out.

Two types of measures are normally used:

- factor yields, determined by the ratio of output volumes to the volumes of individual factors used expressed in physical units, assuming that the conditions of use of every other factor are kept constant;
- unit costs of production, given by the ratio of the amount of resources used expressed in values to the volume of output.

The assessment of efficiency can never be expressed in absolute terms, but must be made through:

- time comparisons, when the efficiency of the same object of observation in different periods is analyzed;
- intercompany comparisons, when the obtained indicator is compared with others from objects similar to the one observed.

In nonprofit organizations, the resources used must be related to outcome measures that are actually representative of the productive mission of the company and therefore of the increase in the well-being status.

4.4 The analysis of technical efficiency: Some observations

Calculating the efficiency ratio is simple if only one input is used in the production process to obtain one output, and if the output is represented by units of physical type products that can be easily quantified. Normally, production processes are characterized by a plurality of inputs and a plurality of outputs. In addition, in nonprofit organizations it is often necessary to detect the output produced in terms of services. If a global indicator is to be used, it is necessary to aggregate all inputs on one side and all outputs on the other. If, on the other hand, one refers to only one factor of production, assuming that the others are all employed at some level, one must speak of partial indicators. The construction of global efficiency indicators makes it possible to compare different production units provided that the units produced and the units of factors employed are identifiable, measurable, and homogeneous with each other (Angeloni & Fiorentini, 1996). The problem of homogenizing inputs and outputs could be overcome by expressing the variables in monetary terms. In nonprofit organizations, however, it is difficult to express output in monetary terms; only inputs can often be quantified by monetary values. When the output produced is represented by services the output measures are not always represented by physical quantities. In this case it is possible to quantify the goods through which the service materializes, or the time employed for the services, or the number of beneficiaries satisfied. Therefore, to measure quantity one can refer to the number of clients/users, when the services offered are not differentiated; if they are differentiated one could refer to the time taken to provide the services, or the number of cases presented within a day, and so on. Indicators that refer to the whole organization often do not take into account the complementarity of factors that are jointly employed in various production processes. The low efficiency of some production processes could be offset by the higher efficiency of other processes. When possible, it would be appropriate to calculate indexes with reference to production processes.

4.5 The partial efficiency performance indicators

We will first analyze which partial efficiency indicators can be applied to nonprofit organizations[2] and then consider how the different indicators can be aggregated to obtain index numbers. Partial efficiency indicators are obtained from the ratio of physical units of output to physical units of homogeneous input used, assuming that all other inputs are constant. The processes that take place in organizations are the result of a combination of factors; therefore, it is essential to know the contribution of each input in obtaining the different products and services. Let us assume that the technical factors that can be used in productions can be distinguished into three fundamental classes:

- labor, both paid and voluntary, denoted by QL;
- materials and other fast-cycle factors, both purchased and donated, denoted by QM;
- installations, including all technical fixed assets, both tangible and intangible, denoted by QI.

If we neglect the quality coefficient[3] of productions, the previous model can be rewritten in the following form: (QL, QM, QI) → Productive transformation → QP

By looking at the model's inputs and outputs, it is possible to express production efficiency with the output ratios, which show the amount of goods or services that the use of each unit of the factor considered allows to be obtained. The output ratios can be identified in the following:

- Labor factor yield $\sigma L = \frac{QP}{QL}$

To quantify the labor factor we usually refer to hours worked (average hourly yield), days worked (daily yield), and the number of employees hired (per capita yield):

- Material factor yield $\sigma L = \frac{QP}{QM}$

To quantify material consumption we can use the unit of measurement corresponding to the physical-technical unit of the materials, kilograms, liters, cubic meters, and so on:

- Plant and Equipment factor yield $\sigma L = \frac{QP}{QI}$

To quantify Plant and Equipment, the unit of measurement could refer to hours of operation (hourly productivity), or the number of services rendered (productivity per kilometer, per press stroke, etc.) (Marchi, Paolini & Quagli, 2003). The numbers obtained are "pure" and indicate how many units of output can be considered achieved for each of the units used in the denominator factor. The ones we have considered are average yield measures and have the characteristic of referring to a defined time period. It is also possible to calculate marginal returns by determining the amount of extra output obtainable by adding a unit of factor in the production process, if the quantities of the other factors are fixed. In some cases an ideal measure of output might be the utility derived to the individual, or to the community as a whole, from an additional unit of service rendered, but calculating this measure poses several challenges. When we do not have consumer goods as outputs, the measurement problem often relates to the fact that the service itself does not increase the utility of the individual, but we derive utility from an increase in the welfare status, for example, from the increase in longevity that the service can bring about. In addition, there is a high degree of variability that can distinguish the outcomes actually produced by the specific service (Angeloni & Fiorentini, 1996). Performance indexes highlight how much production is achieved with one unit of production factor. For process analysis and control, it can be useful to calculate the amount of a given factor that is required to obtain a unit of production. We can obtain this information by calculating the rates of factor use, which are the opposite of the yield indexes:

Labor factor use rate $\rho L = \dfrac{QL}{QP}$

Material factor use rate $\rho M = \dfrac{QM}{QP}$

Plant and Equipment factor use rate $\rho I = \dfrac{QI}{QP}$

Use rates can be employed to analyze the production combination defined as the combination of factors required to obtain the finished product.

4.6 The use of performance indexes for the evaluation of internal efficiency

Yield indexes and factor use rates can be employed in evaluating the internal efficiency of production transformation to observe the process structure and keep track of its efficiency:

- through comparisons of yields in space, among different operation centers, if the yield of a given factor in a given department is higher than that of another, so also the efficiency in using that factor will be higher, given the same other circumstances;

- through comparisons over time, comparisons are made for different periods and for the same center, if the performance of a factor increases over time, similarly the efficiency will progress, given all other conditions being equal; since it is very difficult to isolate the performance of the factor examined from the variations endured by the other factors, the performance of a production factor must be interpreted by analyzing the influence that the variation has exerted on the system of other qualitative and quantitative variables in order to be able to define a more or less efficient production process;

- through comparisons of the actual calculated data for the processes carried out with standard measures of yield, calculated assuming given levels of production efficiency in the use of the various factors; if the calculated yields approach or exceed the pre-calculated standard yields, efficiency will also progress in the same direction;

- through comparisons between production budget data and actual data; if actual yields approach and exceed budget yields, planned efficiency will have been met or exceeded.

4.7 The labor yield

Of all performance indexes, one of the most widely used indicators is the average labor yield, for nonprofit organizations that also produce for the market. The importance attached to the labor factor is even more evident in nonprofit organizations which, while employing material inputs, rely primarily on the energies of the individuals who lend their services. Also called physical labor productivity, it is the commonly understood "productivity". Although it has various designations, it still remains an index of performance as defined above. Let us take up the fundamental expression of labor yield:

$$\text{Labor factor yield } \sigma L = \frac{QP}{QL}$$

If we also consider quality, which always characterizes a production process, the previous ratio will have to be rewritten in a form that also takes into account the quality aspects of production. Suppose we determine a "quality coefficient" of productions and denote it by "qlP". This coefficient will possibly have to be measured in terms of observable characteristics. We can thus write the ratio:

$$\sigma L = \frac{QP \times qlP}{QL}$$

The ratio points out that labor yield depends not only on the efficiency of human operation to obtain given quantities of goods or services, but also on the efficiency of obtaining goods or services of a given quality.

We can increase the yield if:

- with the same QL increases QP, but also when,
- with the same QL and QP increases qlP.

Even the labor presents aspects of quantity and quality. If we suppose that we are capable of quantifying a parameter aimed at expressing the quality of labor and denote it by "qlL". This parameter should be chosen taking into account observable characteristics in terms of:

- learning-related skills;
- composition of workers by gender, educational qualification, age, etc.;
- years of experience;
- physical and psychological conditions in which the work is performed, and so on.

The yield ratio will thus be expanded:

$$\sigma L = \frac{QP \times qlP}{QL/qlL}$$

From this indicator, it appears that the yield indicator may also increase as a result of job quality, all other things being equal. Note that the labor quality coefficient appears as the denominator of the QL/qlL ratio. This solution was chosen because the σL indicator we are analyzing expresses the efficiency of the labor factor, and it seems, therefore, correct to think that the worker seeks to decrease the burden of labor (denominator) for the same results (numerator). The overall burden of work increases the more time is devoted to work, but it decreases the higher the quality of work, considered as the quality of the conditions under which the work is performed. In extreme cases, work becomes "fulfillment" and "joy".

4.8 Staff-based measures

When calculating labor performance, it is necessary to specify whether by the term labor we mean:

*   labor "assigned" to a given production process, whereby labor "assigned" we mean labor theoretically deliverable by all workers employed in that process;
*   labor actually performed, that is, work actually done by only those workers who participated in the production process.

Labor yield, if for simplicity's sake we do not consider quality, can be specified as follows:

*   using the total labor "assigned" to obtain that output we get:

$$\sigma L\ \text{ASS.} = \frac{QP}{QL\ \text{ASS.}}$$

*   using the actual labor employed is obtained:

$$\sigma L\ \text{EMP.} = \frac{QP}{QL\ \text{EMP.}}$$

If N workers are assigned to a given production process, but only M < N work, some labor remains underused or unused, and the output of the labor employed will be greater than that of the labor assigned.

We can also distinguish two categories of workers:

*   paid;
*   volunteers.

The previous indicators could be calculated taking into consideration that the labor employed and the labor assigned are given by the sum of:

$$QL\ \text{ASS.} = QL\ \text{ASS. to employees} + QL\ \text{ASS. to volunteers}$$

QL IMP. = QL EMP. by employees + QL EMP. by volunteers

Regarding the indicators for unpaid work, the main difficulties arise from the following considerations:

* it is not always possible to know the number of "donated" hours;
* it is not always possible to have data on the type and quality of work performed.

The following indexes can be used to assess the breakdown of human resources in nonprofit organizations:

$$\frac{\text{hours of paid work}}{\text{total hoursof work}} \times 100$$

$$\frac{\text{No. of paid workers}}{\text{Total number of workers}} \times 100$$

The one-hundred complement of the previous ratios represents the contribution of volunteers expressed in terms of hours worked out of the total and percentage of volunteer workers out of the total.

Other possible indicators are:

$$\frac{\text{No. of monthly worked hours}}{\text{No. of paid workers}}$$

$$\frac{\text{No. of monthly worked hours}}{\text{No. of volunteers}}$$

An indicator expressing the composition of the labor factor may be as follows:

$$\frac{\text{No. of monthly worked hours}}{\text{No. of paid hours}}$$

In case the indicator is greater than unity it indicates the presence of unpaid work. On the other hand, if it is less than the unit it shows the existence of some degree of absenteeism. However, the two effects could compensate each other and would not be shown separately by the indicator.

4.9 Labor employment intensity

The calculation of the yield of labor employed can also be carried out by expressing it as a function of the yield of labor assigned in the following way:

$$\sigma L \ ASS. = \frac{QP}{QL \ EMP.} \times \frac{QL \ EMP.}{QL \ ASS.}$$

The overall yield assigned to production processes is calculated as a function:

- of the yield of labor actually performed in the production process;
- of the ratio of labor intensity of employment.

The labor employment intensity given by the ratio of:

$$\frac{QL \ EMP.}{QL \ ASS.}$$

Is influenced by:

- absenteeism rate, this indicator expresses the percentage of hours not worked due to justified (illness, maternity, etc.) and unjustified absences;

$$ar \ \% = \frac{hours \ not \ worked \ due \ to \ absences}{hours \ assigned} \times 100$$

- inactivity rate of the production center, this indicator expresses the percentage of hours not worked due to the non-operation of the production center for reasons unrelated to workers such as scheduled maintenance, breakdowns, etc.;

$$ir \ \% = \frac{hours \ not \ worked \ due \ to \ non - operation}{hours \ assigned} \times 100$$

- overabundance rate of labor, this indicator expresses the amount of labor assigned in excess to a production center with respect to demands, this rate expresses incorrect assignment of workers.

$$\text{or } \% = \frac{\text{amount of work assigned in excess}}{\text{amount of work assigned}} \times 100$$

We can now express the amount of labor employed in the following way:

$$\text{QL EMP.} = \text{QL ASS.} \, (100 - ar\%) \, (100 - ir\%) \, (100 - or\%)$$

Then the intensity of labor employment can be expressed by the following formula:

$$\frac{\text{QL IMP.}}{\text{QL ASS.}} = (100 - ar\%) \, (100 - ir\%) \, (100 - or\%)$$

It therefore turns out to be possible to evaluate production efficiency with the following:

$$\sigma\text{L ASS.} = \frac{\text{QP}}{\text{QL EMP.}} (100 - ar\%) a (100 - ir\%)(100 - or\%)$$

which expresses labor performance as a function of actual performance and the factors of absenteeism, inactivity, and overabundance that reduce that output. In cases where it is difficult or impossible to express output in terms of services produced, one indicator of efficiency that can be used is the rate of employment of workers. If we compare two nonprofit organizations operating in the same sector, for the same number of resources employed, the organization with the highest worker employment rate will be more efficient. In indicators where the number of people working in the production process is used, to make the input data homogeneous, it is necessary to express this in terms of full-time equivalence. Indicators expressing the employment of workers in institutional and management activities can also be calculated. One can, for example, calculate the ratio of workers employed per institutional activity to total workers:

$$\frac{\text{workers per institutional activities}}{\text{workers}} \%$$

This indicator requires careful analysis, as a low percentage could indicate excessive bureaucratization of the structure, however, a high percentage could also mean a lack of attention to management and other activities that can still be valuable in achieving goals.

4.10 Composite indexes of labor performance

In order to assess the efficiency of the organization, it is necessary to check whether human labor has been coordinated with mechanical labor, making the best use of machinery and equipment. Labor efficiency can be evaluated by taking into account the available machinery and equipment. We can express the rate at which human labor is employed in relation to machine labor employed as follows:

$$\frac{QL\ EMP.}{Q\ MACH.\ \ EMP.}$$

We can also express the plant utilization rate with respect to the assigned production capacity with the following indicator:

$$\frac{Q\ MACH.\ \ EMP.}{Q\ MACH.\ \ ASS.}$$

Finally, we can express the machine endowment rate for the work actually performed with the ratio:

$$\frac{Q\ MACH.\ \ ASS.}{Q\ L.\ \ ASS.}$$

Using the previous indicators, we can express labor performance with the following equation:

$$\sigma L\ ASS. = \frac{QP}{QL\ EMP.} \times \frac{QL\ EMP.}{Q\ MACH.\ EMP} \times \frac{Q\ MACH.\ EMP}{Q\ MACH.\ ASS.}$$
$$\times \frac{Q\ MACH.\ ASS}{QL\ ASS.}$$

4.11 Quality

Quality represents a fundamental element in the assessment of the efficiency of productive transformation. Quality affects the efficiency of economic transformation and the effectiveness of managerial transformation because it represents the fundamental element on which customer/user appreciation is based. The notion of quality is not easily defined (Mella, 1997). In general, we can distinguish two aspects of quality:

a   extrinsic, use, or functional quality;
b   intrinsic, design, or instrumental quality.

We identify the extrinsic, use, or functional quality if we consider the characteristics that make an object suitable to be used for some purpose or that make a service suitable to satisfy the needs of the subjects for whom they are intended; the functional quality of a product is its aptitude to satisfy the use function required by the community. A product must be meant to satisfy the needs, and thus the demands, of those for whom it is intended, so it will have to be technically useful. In addition to being technically useful, however, it will also have to satisfy needs expressible in terms of aspirations. Indicators that can be used to analyze extrinsic qualities are aimed at identifying:

•   the existence of updated technical characteristics to keep the product or service suitable for satisfying needs;
•   the presence of checks in relation to the needs and aspirations of the community receiving the goods and services.

In nonprofit organizations, indicators related to qualitative aspects obtainable through the collection of subjective judgments tend to take on greater importance than in businesses where market mechanisms provide a kind of automatic control of the quality itself. We identify intrinsic, design, or instrumental quality when we consider characteristics that make an object or service compliant with a reference standard or that define its operation similar to a reference standard. The reference standard may be represented by the products or services offered in the past, in case a time comparison is carried out. Therefore, it will be significant for the intrinsic quality to remain in accordance with set quality standards or improve over time. Indicators related to design quality are aimed at identifying:

•   the preservation of the unified technical standard in space and time;
•   any defects;
•   the existence of a service to carry out inspections and replace, revise, repair faulty products.

By way of example, the following parameters aimed at identifying the greater or lesser quality of products or services may be considered: the reduction of faulty products over time; the decrease in scrap; the adherence to predetermined standards; the speed of service delivery or order fulfillment; the promptness in repairing any faults; and the increase in the degree of customer/user satisfaction. On the basis of these parameters we can build indicators from which a comparative analysis can show the process of improving the quality of the output of production processing.

4.12 Quality analysis

The analysis of faults in a nonprofit organization that manufactures physical goods can be done by comparing at various periods the following ratio:

$$\frac{\text{Number of faulty products}}{\text{Number of products obtained}}$$

The indicator shows the frequency with which faults occur; time analysis of this indicator shows the probability that a product is faulty. Whether the company performs production of goods or services, it is possible to calculate the reduction in scraps. The following indicator can be used:

$$\frac{\text{Volume of scraps}}{\text{Volume of materials used}}$$

Some organizations have prefixed standards concerning the average number of acceptable faulty products or the average amount of permissible scraps. In order to consider indicators associated with the production situation of the company to which they are related, it is possible to use the difference between the measured value and the prefixed standard as the numerator and denominator, respectively, the number of products obtained and the volume of materials used, expressing it as a percentage, as follows:

$$\frac{\text{Number of faulty products} - \text{Standard number of faulty products}}{\text{Number of products obtained}} \times 100$$

$$\frac{\text{Volume of scraps} - \text{Standard volume of scraps}}{\text{Volume of materials used}} \times 100$$

If the result of this indicator is negative, the percentage of faults or scraps is lower than the standard percentage. If the result is positive the company will have lower quality margins than expected. Regarding the speed of order fulfillment or service delivery, indicators can be calculated that express the time required to deliver a good or to render a service. The calculation of waiting times can be very important in companies that deliver services related to the person. However, the absolute value of waiting times may not be sufficient to express the quality level of the service; it would be necessary to set average standard times to be compared at the end of the year. Regarding the degree of customer/user satisfaction, one indicator that can be used is the following:

$$\frac{\text{Number of complaints}}{\text{Total number of users}}$$

This indicator can be significant when analyzed in conjunction with some physical-technical efficiency indicators. A high output of production factors causes a real improvement in business efficiency only if the higher volume of output obtained with each unit of production factor has not been achieved at the expense of the quality of performance. Indicators that are based on the degree of customer/user satisfaction are derived from the statements made by service recipients, and are therefore unable to provide objective assessments. They are also determined in a context of information asymmetries and therefore difficult to evaluate (Angeloni & Fiorentini, 1996). For the purpose of appreciation, distinguishing "customer-perceived" quality from quality objectively measured by company managers is desirable. When it is difficult or impossible to measure output in evaluating the quality of services provided one indicator that is often used is the qualification of personnel employed. Thus an indirect indicator of quality is constructed based more on the characteristics of inputs than outputs. The presence and quality of certain figures important for the purpose of production of goods and provision of services signals the orientation of the nonprofit company toward excellence. These elements can be measured with a nominal scale in which variables can take the value "yes" or "no". One quality (Khumawala, Parsons & Gordon, 2005) indicator that can be employed is the full-time staff utilization rate per client/user; this indicator can also be calculated by referring to qualified staff:

$$\frac{\text{Contributors per institutional activities}}{\text{users}}$$

$$\frac{\text{Qualified staff}}{\text{users}}$$

Both indicators provide information on the quantitative adequacy of the human resources employed, the second also expresses the quality of the service provided. Note that the meaning attributable to the adjective "qualified" varies in relation to sectors and job positions. Other indicators take into consideration the staff composition by highlighting the percentage of qualified staff out of the total:

$$\frac{\text{Qualified staff}}{\text{staff}}\%$$

The indicator reports the company's ability to provide quality service. To assess the quality standard, it is possible to refer to quality standards that can be based on:

- the past experience of the organization itself;
- the observation of organization carrying out the activity in the same industry;
- regulatory provisions.[4]

Quality standards can be represented:

- by a single value such as the time required to provide a certain service;
- by ratios between two values, normally a measure of the absolute quality level of services is used in the numerator and the number of beneficiaries in the denominator; an attempt is made to express the indicator in terms of service per capita.

4.13 Improper yields

When we calculate performance indicators we express inputs and outputs in quantitative terms. However, there are some inputs that cannot be expressed in nonmonetary quantities. Some expenses incurred in the acquisition of services, such as transportation, advertising, insurance, consulting, etc., can hardly be expressed in nonmonetary quantities; the only measure that can express their use is currency. These factors also have another peculiarity: their use is not always directly functional to production in the strict sense, but they contribute indirectly to the execution of the organization's activities and the achievement of its objectives. The calculation of the yields of these factors can be made only by employing their values, which is why these yields are called "improper" (Guatri, 1950). For those factors that are not directly related to the organization's production volume, the improper output should be calculated by considering as output the volume of the phenomenon it originated.

$$\text{Improper yield} = \frac{\text{Volume of the "phenomenon"}}{\text{Amount of factor employed}}$$

If the input whose performance is being analyzed is not the only variable capable of influencing the phenomenon under consideration it will also be necessary to consider "influence variables" in the analysis. The partial efficiency indicators we have examined have the shortcoming of not being able to capture the joint effects of the production factors. To overcome this problem, it is possible to use global indicators that refer to all inputs used and all outputs obtained, or to proceed to the aggregation of partial indicators. To do this, homogeneous data must be used. In a nonprofit organization it is difficult, if not impossible, to express output in monetary terms so it is preferable to refer to physical units of goods and services offered. However, cost indicators that express the cost required to produce a physical unit of output can be used. Thus an alternative technical efficiency indicator can be given by the relationship between the quantity produced (QP) and the cost of factors of production (CF):

$$\text{Overall technical efficiency} = \frac{QP}{CF}$$

This indicator is only applicable if it can be presumed that all operational units pursue the goal of minimizing production costs.

4.14 Economic efficiency

To analyze economic efficiency, we revisit the interpretation of the nonprofit organization as an economic transformer according to Figure 2.8. In the organization considered as a system of economic transformation, economic efficiency can be emphasized, which we have already defined as the system's ability to maximize the cost-effectiveness ratio:

$$E = \frac{\text{Value of output productions}}{\text{Value of input factors}}$$

Economic efficiency can also be expressed through the inverse of the cost-effectiveness ratio, which is called the cost rate or also CPC (Cost Per Cent):

$$CPC = \frac{\text{Value of input factors}}{\text{Value of output productions}}$$

CPC indicates how many monetary units of cost are required for each monetary unit of production value. Economic transformation is more efficient the higher E is and the lower CPC is. The problem that needs to be addressed is to quantify the positive externalities produced by the management of nonprofit organizations. To solve this problem, it is necessary to broaden the definition of cost-effectiveness. The nonprofit organization must produce value, or wealth, but it does not necessarily have to be financial wealth. Cost-effectiveness (affordability), as defined in Section 3.5, is considered to be:

- the ability over time to adequately remunerate the factors of production employed;[5]
- the "creation of value" (Ashton, 2005; Freudenreich, Lüdeke-Freund & Schaltegger, 2020; Groth & Kinney, 1994; Low, 2000).

Expressions are used to convey the ability of organizations to pursue over time the objectives for which they were founded. In order to examine the conditions under which organizations exist over time, it is necessary to analyze the company's ability to last over time (Zappa, 1956). In the survival of such organizations, the intervention of the community in which they operate plays a key role, which can be implemented directly through voluntary contributions and indirectly through the public body. The community obtains:

- a direct social benefit from the activity of such organizations;
- but also an indirect economic benefit, which, however, is often difficult to assess.[6]

4.15 The analysis of economic efficiency: External and internal efficiency

Onida speaking of the public company, but the point can also be extended to nonprofit organizations, argues that "the utmost care must be taken to ensure cost-effectiveness, understood as efficiency, employing the highest yield of the necessary and convenient factors and production processes, eliminating all waste, reducing to a minimum, the costs to be incurred in order to achieve the ends assigned to the organization. To produce without profit, indeed, does not mean ... to produce badly and without regard to the cost and operating losses that the community is called upon, directly or indirectly, to bear" (Onida, 1971, p. 95). The organization's activity can be defined as economically viable if it allows for the achievement of economic equilibrium and if it achieves the general purposes that the organization aims at. The general objectives of management can be identified in the achievement of institutional purposes with the presence of positive components aimed at replenishing survival costs and allowing institutional costs to expand as much as possible under efficient conditions. The use of indicators of productive transformation, which are of physical-technical nature, does not allow for a complete analysis of business efficiency, as they do not take into account magnitudes in monetary terms. The cost-effectiveness ratio, which expresses the efficiency of economic transformation, can be investigated operationally to understand what are the managerial conditions of cost-effectiveness and what are the typical ways to achieve it in a nonprofit. The value of productions in Output, for nonprofit organizations that sell productions in the market, can be rewritten as the product of the quantity of products by the selling price (QP × pS) and the same can also be done for the value of factors in Input (QF × pP), the previous ratio can be broken down as follows:

$$E = \frac{\text{Value of productions}}{\text{Value of factors}} = \frac{QP \times pS}{QF \times pP} = \frac{QP}{QF} \times \frac{pS}{pP}$$

The first of the two final quotients represents the productivity ratio aimed at expressing the productive or internal efficiency that characterizes productive transformation, also called negotiation efficiency. The second quotient is the price ratio expressing the organization's ability to negotiate productions in target markets and factors in supply markets, which might be referred to as negotiation or external efficiency. Economic transformation depends on productive transformation and the organization's ability to negotiate. The latter is a variable on which it is difficult to act. External management cannot be regarded only in relation to sales price formation, but associated with it are also the negotiations of purchase and sales volumes. External efficiency should be observed in relation to the ability to expand the volume of goods and services offered. Internal efficiency should be calculated by making sure that the volumes used in the numerator are closely related to the volumes of factors used. Maximizing internal and external efficiency maximizes cost-effectiveness.

Efficiency E depends on two factors:

- QP/QF which is an indicator (prevailing) of internal efficiency;
- pS/pP which is an indicator (prevailing) of external efficiency.

Cost-effectiveness can be considered a function of both internal efficiency and external efficiency of management. An increase in efficiency, all other things being equal, allows an increase in the cost-effectiveness indicator. To increase cost-effectiveness, there are two possibilities:

- achieve cost-effectiveness through the combination efficiency index;
- achieve cost-effectiveness through the negotiation efficiency index.

In nonprofit organizations that succeed in the market, in which market-price revenues prevail, one can certainly consider negotiation efficiency as well. It usually happens that nonprofit organizations, which do not have the power to negotiate prices because they operate in sectors in which there is no market, will therefore have to rationalize as much as possible the degree of internal efficiency related to the structure of production transformation processes.

4.16 Cost-effectiveness (affordability) conditions

In analyzing the cost-effectiveness of the nonprofit organization, it should be kept in mind that economic transformation does not aim to maximize revenues, but aims to satisfy customers/users regarding the quality and quantity of products and services made available. Therefore, in order to achieve a good level of cost-effectiveness, it will be necessary to consider the quantity of resources used and the quantity and quality of products and services rendered.

The internal efficiency indicator will have to be completed in this way:

$$\frac{QP \times qlP}{QA}$$

The degree of cost-effectiveness is related to the degree to which extra-economic purposes are achieved and the resources allocated to their pursuit. Cost-effectiveness is specific to any nonprofit organization and is determined by the multiple institutional and noninstitutional interests that flow into the organization.

The achievement of cost-effectiveness must take into account:

- the conditions of operation;
- of the environment that may define the scope of action.

In order to succeed in assessing the degree of cost-effectiveness of a nonprofit organization, one would have to point out the conditions without which there is not an acceptable level of cost-effectiveness of management, knowing that these conditions will have to be combined with others of a subjective nature, on the acceptability of the allocation of resources and the response to institutional expectations (Borzaga, Fiorentini & Matacena, 1996).

The necessary conditions might be as follows:

- economic balance;
- customer/user satisfaction with the quantity/quality of products and services and the functions performed with respect to objectives.

Economic equilibrium is linked to the ability to sufficiently remunerate all the factors employed, both tangible and intangible factors that enable the company to last over time. Economic balance depends not only on the ability to acquire the necessary production factors, but also to build up adequate assets that enable the company to grow. The second condition can be achieved through the organization's ability to fulfill its production process and perform functions in line with its purpose in terms of quantity and quality. The organization's ability to achieve goals can be called managerial effectiveness. The criterion of cost-effectiveness makes it possible to analyze whether or not it is worthwhile to start and continue a business activity, it does not define the causes behind it. Therefore, the other indicators of efficiency and effectiveness should be used. Efficiency and effectiveness are conditions of cost-effectiveness, they explain its cause and make it possible to identify the tools to be operated to improve its level. The lack of a market on which to observe price formation makes it difficult to use this value, while the acquisition of production factors, in most cases, takes place in the same markets in which the organizations operate. In nonprofit organizations in which it is difficult or impossible to express output in monetary terms, it will be appropriate to refer to the physical units of goods and services offered. However, cost indicators that express the cost required to produce a unit of output can be used. In nonprofit organizations, the current value, in case it is identifiable, of the goods and services normally rendered does not represent a rational and objective measure of the consistency, monetary and, otherwise, of disbursements. Indicators designed to show the ratio of actual revenues to total costs, or of fee revenues to total costs, could be used, but their reliability for the purpose of detecting the degree of efficiency would be poor. In cases where the inputs include resources acquired free of charge, such factors could be evaluated on the basis of the current prices of similar factors.

4.17 Economic productivity indicators

To analyze economic transformation, it is possible to refer to global indicators that express the average total cost per unit of output. As we have already mentioned, given the difficulty of expressing output in monetary terms, measures designed to highlight physical units are used. Should this also be difficult, substitute measures of their volume may be used, but aimed at quantifying them rationally and objectively. A meaningful indicator would be to calculate average charges per unit of service delivered:

$$\text{average charges per unit disbursed} = \frac{\text{total charges}}{\text{volume of disbursements}}$$

The numerator conveys the total costs incurred for the production process and the delivery of the good or service (Waterhouse, 1992). This indicator represents an overall measure of productivity. Partial measures could also be calculated by referring to the amount of costs incurred for each individual factor of production. One could, for example, calculate the cost of the labor factor per unit of product or user:

$$\frac{\text{Direct staff costs}}{\text{Volume of disbursements}}$$

Another partial indicator could take into account the breakdown of total costs into management costs and institutional costs.

$$\frac{\text{total charges}}{\text{Volume of disbursements}} = \frac{\text{management costs} + \text{institutional costs}}{\text{Volume of disbursements}}$$

The denominator measures the volume of disbursements. To identify it correctly, it is essential to have a stream of detailed information about the goods and services disbursed. Some measures that can be used are the following:

- the number of users, when it is possible to numerically identify the individuals who have used the goods or services provided in a given reference period;
- the number of members, when the nonprofit organization provides services to members upon payment of a membership fee;
- the number of days or hours of service delivery, when service deliveries are made continuously and it is not possible to identify the average number of users since each user receives a certain form of assistance at irregular intervals of time.

4.18 Financial efficiency

The third group of efficiency indicators is the one emerging from financial transformation: the financial efficiency indicators. The model of a company as a financial transformer is in Figure 2.11. The nonprofit organization in addition to being a financial transformer can also be regarded as an investment center that collects money and invests it productively; in this way, invested capital is formed, which is quantitatively equal to the capital raised by the organization given by the sum of capital invested by the promoters, contributions, and passive funding:

$$IC = RC + C + LC$$

Management implements the productive investment of IC; the resources acquired through contributions are invested for the purchase of production factors and for the implementation of processes; through the sale of goods or the provision of services, the monetary resources invested are recovered and, if the economic transformation has been positive, the disinvestment allows the organization to obtain a distinctive economic result through which to remunerate any capital raised by way of loans (remunerated with Passive Interest) and to obtain an operating surplus through which to self-finance the activity and thus increase the capital available. One can then write:

$$\text{Distinctive economic result} = IP + \text{Operating surplus}$$

It can be observed that the distinctive economic result is divided into two parts: passive interest, representing the financial remuneration of the capital invested in the organization by way of loan, and the operating surplus, which represents the eventual and residual result of the capital contributed by the founders and donors, who do not pursue the goal of receiving remuneration, but that of seeing the objectives of the organization achieved. Looking at the above two equations simultaneously, it can be seen that:

- the characteristic economic result represents the remuneration obtained by the enterprise for the productive investment of the invested capital IC;
- passive interest represents the remuneration of the capital invested in the organization by lenders in the form of passive financing;
- operating surplus expresses the ability of the nonprofit organization to finance itself.

4.19 Financial efficiency indicators

If we now go back to looking at the nonprofit organization as a financial transformation system that presents in input the capital invested and in output the results obtained, it is easy to derive the three financial efficiency ratios:

$$\frac{\text{Distinctive economic output result}}{\text{Invested input capital}}$$

The first indicator shows the unit return on capital invested by the company, in other words, the return obtained by the company in order to allow the return on capital invested in it by external parties and to obtain self-funding. The value of this quotient acquires little significance in the case where the organization has developed the activity of economic support. In this case, the distinctive economic result should be analyzed at the level of the single relevant activities.

$$\frac{\text{Passive output interests}}{\text{Passive input fundings}}$$

The second quotient indicates financial efficiency by calculating the unit rate of return on financing obtained by the organization. For the organization, it represents the financial cost of capital obtained as a loan. For lenders, it represents a rate of return on borrowed capital.

$$\frac{\text{Operating output surplus}}{\text{Capital from promoters + Input contributions}}$$

The third indicator expresses financial efficiency in terms of unit rate of return on equity and contributions. This indicator does not possess the signaling value it assumes in businesses because this quotient is not a response to the expectations of an important category of corporate stakeholders. In nonprofit organizations, capital is given not only by promoters but also by donors. It may be of interest to analyze the composition of capital with the following indicator:

$$\frac{RC + C}{IC}$$

This indicator represents the incidence of contributions and the ability of the nonprofit organization to obtain funds to be used in productive resources without the corresponding use of financing sources aggravating current expenses by incurring financial charges. Another financial indicator that can be used is the debt indicator given by the ratio of loans payable to equity:

$$\frac{LC}{RC}$$

It expresses the organization's ability to sustainably fuel its operation without stretching its reliance on debt financing beyond an acceptable threshold. It can also be rewritten by considering capital obtained from promoters and donors in the denominator:

$$\frac{LC}{RC + C}$$

Efficiency indicators, while highly important, show nothing about the realization of the purposes for which the nonprofit organization was set up and which had motivated the investment of capital by promoters and donors.

Notes

1 Velo (1995), talking about the nonprofit's future, argues: "Nonprofit organizations are increasingly required to shift from a product-oriented rationale, based on simple service delivery, to a market-oriented rationale, aimed at efficiently delivering quality performance".

2 Some authors have pointed out that the characteristics of immateriality, which often characterizes the output of nonprofit organizations, make it difficult to calculate the returns on the factors employed (Kanter, 1979; Anthony & Young, 1988; Chansky, Garner & Raichoudhary, 2016).

3 The quality of the output of the production process will be analyzed in the next chapter with the measurement of the degree of customer/user satisfaction.

4 Consider, for example, a quality indicator for education and training companies: the number of pupils per teacher. The maximum number is set by law. Another significant example we can point out is the quality standards of certain services set by the European Economic Community with UNI standards.

5 Cost-effectiveness (affordability) is to be understood as the ability over time to adequately remunerate the production factors employed in order to allow the regeneration of the resources originally invested and to remain in the market (Paolone & D'Amico, 1994, p. 36).

6 Consider the case where a nonprofit organization performs the task of creating jobs for disabled people (Andreaus, 1997). Its productivity would never be comparable to that of a business offering the same products in the market. The nonprofit would have to sell at market prices even though it would not get to cover its costs in this way. If we interpreted the concept of cost-effectiveness narrowly, this organization could not exist because it lacks the proper conditions of existence. The community, however, gets two benefits from this activity:

- a direct benefit related to the fact that disabled people if they did not work in the nonprofit organization would have to receive an allowance from the community;
- an indirect benefit determined by the fact that those who receive an allowance without producing, if in possession of a minimum of self-awareness, are in a state of frustration that could cause dangerous social tensions.

Reference list

Airoldi, G., Brunetti, G., & Coda, V. (2020). *Corso di economia aziendale*. Bologna: Il mulino.

Alves, S., & Andersen, H. T. (2019). *The social and non-profit rental sectors in Portugal and Denmark: Issues of supply, housing quality, and affordability*. In *Housing Policy and Tenure Types in the 21st century: A Southern European perspective* (pp. 73–108). Pisa University Press.

Andreaus, M. (1997). *Un modello di osservazione economico-aziendale per le aziende nonprofit*. Borzaga C., Fiorentini G., Matacena A., Non profit e sistemi di welfare, Roma: NIS.

Angeloni, L., & Fiorentini, G. (1996). *Analisi di efficienza per organizzazioni non profit*. Borzaga C., Fiorentini G., Matacena A. (a cura di), Non profit e sistemi di welfare. Roma: Il contributo della analisi economica, La Nuova Italia Scientifica.

Anthony, R. N., & Young, D. W. (1988). *Management control in non-profit organizations*. Illinois: IRWIN, Homewood.

Ashton, R. H. (2005). Intellectual capital and value creation: A review. *Journal of Accounting Literature, 24*, 53.

Borzaga, C., Fiorentini, G., & Matacena, A. (Eds.). (1996). *Non-profit e sistemi di welfare: Il contributo dell'analisi economica.* La Nuova Italia Scientifica.

Capaldo, P. (1996). *Le aziende non profit: Definizioni e classificazioni. Aa. Vv., Le aziende non profit tra stato e mercato.* Bologna: Atti del convegno Aidea, Clueb.

Chansky, B., Garner, C., & Raichoudhary, R. (2016). Measuring output and productivity in private hospitals. In A. Aizcorbe, C. Baker, E. Berndt, and D. Cutler (Eds.) *Measuring and modeling health care costs* (pp. 145–172). University of Chicago Press.

Freudenreich, B., Lüdeke-Freund, F., & Schaltegger, S. (2020). A stakeholder theory perspective on business models: Value creation for sustainability. *Journal of Business Ethics, 166*(1), 3–18.

Gholamhossein, M., Ali, G. M., & Safdar, A. (2012). An investigation of cost, revenue and profit efficiency: The case of Iranian companies. *African Journal of Business Management, 6*(30), 8879–8888.

Groth, J. C., & Kinney, M. R. (1994). Cost management and value creation. *Management Decision, 32*(4), 52–57.

Guatri, L. (1950). *I rendimenti.* Milano: Giuffrè.

Kanter, R. M. (1979). *The measurement of organizational effectiveness, productivity, performance and success: Issues and dilemmas in service and nonprofit organizations* (No. 8). Institution for Social and Policy Studies, Yale University.

Kanter, R. M., & Summers, D. V. (1994). Doing well while doing good: Dilemmas of performance measurement in nonprofit organizations and the need for a multiple-constituency approach. *Public Sector Management: Theory, Critique and Practice, 220*, 236.

Khumawala, S. B., Parsons, L. M., & Gordon, T. P. (2005). Assessing the quality of not-for-profit efficiency ratios: Do donors use joint cost allocation disclosures?. *Journal of Accounting, Auditing & Finance, 20*(3), 287–309.

Low, J. (2000). The value creation index. *Journal of Intellectual Capital, 1*(3), 252–262.

Marchi, L., Paolini, A., & Quagli, A. (2003). *Strumenti di analisi gestionale.* Torino: Giappichelli.

McConville, D., & Cordery, C. (2021). Not-for-profit performance reporting: A reflection on methods, results and implications for practice and regulation. *VOLUNTAS: International Journal of Voluntary and Nonprofit Organizations*, 1–7.

Mehar, A. (2005). The financial repercussion of cost, revenue and profit: An extension in the BEP and CVP analysis. *Applied Financial Economics, 15*(4), 259–271.

Mella, P. (1992). *Economia aziendale.* Torino: Utet.

Mella, P. (1997). *Dai Sistemi al pensiero sistemico: Per capire i sistemi e pensare con i sistemi* (Vol. 28). Milano: FrancoAngeli.

Mella P. (2008). Systems Thinking e System Dynamics. L'arte di capire la dinamica ed il controllo dei sistemi. Economia Aziendale 2000 Web (ISSN:1826-4719), *4/2008*, 153–192.

Mella P. (2012a). *Systems thinking. Intelligence in action.* New York, Dordrecht, London: Springer.

Mella, P. (2012b). Performance indicators in business value-creating organizations. *Economia Aziendale Online, 2*(2), 25–52.

Mella P. (2014). *Teoria del controllo. dal systems thinking ai sistemi di controllo* (pp. 1–408). Milano: Franco Angeli.

Mella P. (2017). The unexpected cybernetics life of collectivities. *The Combinatory Systems Approach. Kybernetes, 46* (7), 1086–1111.

Mella, P. (2021a, 1st Ed. 2014). *The magic ring. Systems thinking approach to control systems* (Second Edition). Switzerland: Springer Nature.

Mella, P. (2021b). Entrepreneurial dynamics and clusters formation. *The Combinatory Systems View. Economia Aziendale Online, 12*(1), 99–124.

Mella, P. (2022). Global warming: Is it (im)possible to stop it? The systems thinking approach. *Energies, 15*(705), 1–33.

Mella, P., & Gazzola, P. (2019). Improving managers' intelligence through systems thinking. *Kybernetes, 48*(1), 58–78.

Mella, P., & Rangone, A. (2019). Obstacles to managing dynamic systems. The systems thinking approach. *International Journal of Business and Social Science, 10*(8), 24–41.

Mohan, S., Gopalakrishnan, M., & Mizzi, P. J. (2013). Improving the efficiency of a non-profit supply chain for the food insecure. *International Journal of Production Economics, 143*(2), 248–255.

Molteni, M. M. (1997). *Le misure di performance nelle aziende non profit di servizio alla persona.* Padova: Cedam.

Nunamaker, T. R. (1985). Using data envelopment analysis to measure the efficiency of non-profit organizations: A critical evaluation. *Managerial and Decision Economics, 6*(1), 50–58.

Onida, P. (1971). *Economia d'azienda.* Torino: Utet.

Paolone, G., & D'Amico, L. (1994). *L'economia aziendale nei suoi principi parametrici e modelli applicativi.* Torino: Giappichelli.

Ponikvar, N., Tajnikar, M., & Pušnik, K. (2009). Performance ratios for managerial decision-making in a growing firm. *Journal of Business Economics and Management, 10*(2), 109–120.

Rosko, M., Al-Amin, M., & Tavakoli, M. (2020). Efficiency and profitability in US not-for-profit hospitals. *International Journal of Health Economics and Management, 20*(4), 359–379.

Tarigan, N. P. (2012). Managing the nonprofit organization versus the theory and practice of leadership (Peter F. Drucker vs Peter Northouse). *International Journal of Humanities and Applied Sciences (IJHAS), 1*, 117–125.

Travaglini, C. (1992). *Valutazioni e indicatori dei servizi prodotti nelle organizzazioni non profit.* Azienda pubblica. 2.

Usai, G. (1990). *L'efficienza nelle organizzazioni.* Torino: Utet.

Velo, D. (1995). *L'evoluzione del non-profit nel quadro della riforma del Welfare State.* relazione presentata al XVIII Convegno Nazionale AIDEA, Roma.

Waterhouse, J. (1992). Discussion of "Towards a framework for not-for-profit accounting". *Contemporary Accounting Research*, 8(2), 504–508.

Zappa, G. (1956). *Le produzioni nell'economia delle imprese: tomo primo.* Milano: Giuffrè.

5 Sustainability Reporting, Integrated Reporting, and External Performance Indicators: The Exogenous Teleonomy

5.1 The principle of effectiveness in man's activity

If we take again Figure 4.1 relating to man's goal-oriented activity, we can identify the effectiveness indicator:

$$\text{effectiveness} = \frac{\text{extent of satisfaction obtained}}{\text{expected levels of satisfaction (goals)}}$$

Considering again the rationality principle, which underlies human actions, we imagine that individuals operate not only to maximize efficiency but also to maximize the effectiveness of their actions, seeking to maximize the satisfaction achievable with those levels of efficiency. Effectiveness refers to the ability to achieve set goals (Ahmed Alarussi, 2021; Drucker, 1963; Kasim, Haracic & Haracic, 2018; Mouzas, 2006). This term expresses the correspondence between an action and a model used to indicate the goodness of the result itself (Usai, 1990). An organization can be judged effective in relation to the results achieved without taking into account the resources used to achieve those results. Effectiveness can be measured provided that:

- the goals to be achieved can be expressed in measurable terms;
- there's the ability to measure the result actually achieved in order to compare it with the goal.

It should also be borne in mind that:

- the criterion of effectiveness depends on the culture and the system of preferences that lead to positioning the main objectives for the action of the nonprofit organization;

DOI: 10.4324/9781003350439-6

- effectiveness goals vary over time as each stage of the company's life presents specific problems and thus peculiar goals that involve the use of appropriate measures (Kanter & Stein, 1979).

5.2 The choice of objectives

When we observe the process through which entrepreneurial transformation develops, we consider the procedure by which the decision-making, execution, and the supervision of management operations are reached. Entrepreneurial transformation takes place according to the pattern in Figure 2.12. Managerial transformation can be evaluated through the analysis of the effectiveness determined by the ratio

$$\text{effectiveness} = \frac{\text{Output}}{\text{goals}}$$

The main problems encountered in applying this indicator are:

- the quantification of the output, especially in the case of a service, a problem we already addressed in the previous paragraphs;
- the determination of the goals to be achieved.

Therefore, it is not possible to measure the degree of effectiveness if the objectives that are to be achieved have not been set beforehand. For a better understanding it is necessary to think that any activity can be triggered by causes or goals and can be conditioned by constraints. A cause represents an event external to the subject and independent of his or her will upon the occurrence of which a given activity takes place. A goal represents the purpose that the subject intends to achieve and represents the motivation for carrying out the activity. Constraints represent physical, economic, and social conditions that it is not possible or convenient to eliminate. Activities, whether caused or finalized, are the result of a rational calculation that develops in a process that we might call "decision-making". Through this process we implement the conscious choice of one among several possible alternatives to achieve a goal. In order to reach a choice, it is necessary to develop a series of interrelated acts, a process that develops in the following stages:

a   identify objectives to be achieved or those for which problems arise in achieving them,[1] determine the degree of urgency of different objectives and problems;

b   identify the possible alternatives for achieving the objectives;
c   identify the variables that cannot be controlled by the decision-maker and that could influence the achievable results; these variables may be of different kinds:

  •   some of them can be considered real constraints, i.e., environmental conditions that cannot be changed as needed;
  •   other variables may depend on the decisions of other subjects.

d   establish the selection criteria for evaluating each alternative in relation to the possibility of achieving the objective;
e   determine in a predictive way the likely outcomes of the different alternatives, taking into account the constraints;
f   compare the alternatives and choose the one deemed preferable.

5.3 Goals in nonprofit organizations

A performance measure requires that the frame of reference be aimed at identifying the goals that the company aims to achieve. To address this issue, it is necessary to point out that nonprofit organizations can be considered from two aspects:

  •   as instrumental systems;
  •   as directional systems.

They are instrumental systems in that they represent the instruments through which man carries out the basic economic activities of production, consumption, saving and investment of wealth. They are directional systems because they can be considered units with an independent existence with respect to the individuals who participate in them. With the help of the management they can internally design a system of goals and can develop an evolution to achieve them. The ultimate goal of nonprofit organizations, understood as an instrumental system, is to enable the maximum fulfillment of the goals of stakeholders. The organization's activities are aimed at meeting the needs and expectations of various stakeholders (Abzug & Webb, 1999; Crawford, Morgan & Cordery, 2018; Krashinsky, 1997; Minahan & Inglis, 2005), that is, categories of stakeholders, which can be summarized as follows:

  •   meet the needs of both explicit and implicit customers/users, taking into account all those who can benefit from them;
  •   satisfy the expectations of the initiating party constituted by the nucleus that has set up and governs the organization;

- valuing and satisfying both paid and volunteer employees;
- meet the expectations of other stakeholders from whom the company receives natural, human, and financial resources that play a decisive role in survival and development, with special emphasis on public and private entities that make contributions to the organization.

We can call "institutional" the highest goals set for companies as instrumental systems. Organizations can continue to exist only if they succeed in satisfying institutional goals, thus maintaining the conditions of endogenous teleonomy. Therefore, the fulfillment of institutional goals not only represents the ultimate goal, but represents a condition of existence that allows the organization to have lasting life. Institutional purposes represent goals, but at the same time, they also represent constraints on the operation of business entities. A nonprofit organization will have as a condition of existence the fulfillment of the expectations of:

- customers/users through the production of goods or provision of services at levels deemed satisfactory, of adequate quality and as cheap as possible;
- initiating subjects, expectations that may be of different kinds: of esteem, self-actualization, satisfaction of others' needs, etc., related to the fact that the nonprofit organization arises from the initiative of people motivated by philanthropic, religious, cultural intentions, and who make a personal commitment with their own labor and financial resources; the organization is the instrument to drive the dissemination of ethical values, the development of culture, science, or art, to provide assistance to people in need;
- employees, offering adequate monetary remuneration, if they are paid, and fulfilling at best their aspirations, both in the case of paid workers and in the case of voluntary employees; these organizations are based on a pronounced ethical motivation that allows them to avail themselves of the free, voluntary commitment of people who are aimed at ensuring that their ideas are implemented;
- other stakeholders from whom the company receives natural, human, and financial resources, especially the public and private entities that make contributions to the organization, the organization becomes the instrument for the fulfillment of man's need to see certain ideals of life fulfilled, to contribute to the improvement of the society to which they belong, to help their fellow human beings in difficulty.

In order to achieve institutional goals, however, the governing parties must endow the organization itself with specific objectives that are capable of constituting effective guidance for the finalized action carried out. The specific objectives set by the governing parties to the organizations themselves, interpreted as directional systems, can be called directional goals.

5.4 Meeting the expectations of different stakeholders

Performance measurement is analyzed from an external perspective by considering the nonprofit organization in its manifestations of existence and thus in terms of its ability to survive in the environment in which it carries out its institutional activities, and by bringing out the conditions of exogenous teleonomy of such organizations. Nonprofit organizations thus create economic value through user satisfaction, seeking to generate value for the user. The performance of these companies therefore is characterized not only by efficiency factors, but also by qualitative and intangible elements of effectiveness. The result of their operation should not be evaluated in relation to the increase in wealth, as measured by the contrast of exchange values (price-revenue and price-cost), or by the size of the wealth that can be distributed among those who have contributed to production, but in relation to the quantity and quality of needs satisfied, that is, the "utility" produced (Borgonovi, 1995). The contributions that the community makes indirectly through public grants or directly through contributions, donations, and volunteer work can be considered as a kind of monetization of the positive externalities produced by the management of the nonprofit organization (Handy & Brudney, 2007). Nonprofit organizations if they operate according to efficiency criteria allow the increase of collective welfare through the satisfaction of beneficiaries' needs. Performance measures based on physical-quantitative indicators must be supplemented with qualitative ones. Quality indicators tend to be more important than in a company with expectations of return on capital. In the latter, market mechanisms allow for quality control, while in nonprofit organizations lacking this control mechanism, it is necessary to find alternative evaluation criteria (Drucker, 1994).

5.5 Operational effectiveness and economic effectiveness

In order to achieve institutional goals, the nonprofit organization will need to set operational goals. Various objectives may be decided upon during planning:

- a given volume of goods and services to be produced and delivered in a given period of time;
- a given value of average costs per user not to be exceeded in service delivery;
- a given number of subjects to be served in a given period of time.

Effectiveness indicators can be distinguished into two categories:

- operational effectiveness indicators;
- economic effectiveness indicators.

The former compare a planned objective or output expressed in terms of quantities to an actual result or output expressed in the same quantities. Economic effectiveness indicators are obtained by relating actual costs incurred to the level of planned target costs. Some indicators of operational effectiveness might be as follows:

$$\frac{\text{Quantity of actual goods or services}}{\text{Quantity of goods or services planned}}$$

This indicator can be used when the company's goal is to deliver a given quantity of goods or services, regardless of the number of beneficiaries who use them.

$$\frac{\text{Number of actual users}}{\text{Number of planned users}}$$

This indicator can be used when the goal is to serve a programmed number of users. However, it would be useful to monitor not only the number of users actually served, but also the number of "satisfied" users. In other words, it would be interesting to know the number of beneficiaries for whom the provision process, in addition to being activated, was also concluded resulting in the satisfaction of the users' needs.

$$\frac{\text{Quantity of actual goods or services per user}}{\text{Quantity of goods or services planned per user}}$$

This quotient can be employed in cases where the company aims to distribute to each of the beneficiaries served, a given volume of goods or services. Economic effectiveness indicators could be exemplified as follows:

$$\frac{\text{Total actual costs}}{\text{Total programmed costs}}$$

This indicator takes into account the total costs incurred in the company in a given period, which are compared to the total programmed costs. A similar indicator can be built by taking into account only the institutional costs associated with the activity of producing and providing goods and services, both actual and planned ones. If this indicator takes value > 1 it means that the actual costs incurred exceeded the planned ones, the existence of a gap shows ineffective management. If this indicator takes value < 1 the planned costs exceeded the actual costs, it could denote improper planning or an increase in the efficiency of inputs that allowed some business costs to be cut. If this indicator takes value = 1 actual costs were equal to planned costs; this does not necessarily imply that management was effective because the company may have delivered goods or services to fewer actual beneficiaries than planned.

$$\frac{\text{Actual average costs}}{\text{Average programmed costs}}$$

This indicator considers average actual costs compared to planned costs, with average costs understood as the amount of total costs for each of the company's users or beneficiaries.

5.6 Improving user welfare

In order to check the degree of user satisfaction, it is necessary to analyze the achievement of the goal of improving the welfare status of the target subjects.[2] This goal is relevant because it is also a factor directly related to meeting the expectations of other stakeholder categories: promoters, donors, paid employees, and volunteers. Satisfaction results from the gap between quantities that are difficult to define:

- the user's expectations regarding the service, subjective and changing quantities related to personal needs, past experience, information received from other users, and messages sent by the organization externally;
- the user's perception of the service, which is related to various factors, including noncorporate factors; one can consider, for example, the user's perception of variation in the state of welfare, relations with staff and other users, professionalism of staff, technical characteristics, comfort of the physical facility, accessibility, etc.

Measuring improvement in the state of welfare is difficult to carry out. It requires the help of various scientific disciplines such as sociology, psychology, medicine, etc. Each discipline has developed survey instruments to measure a person's state of welfare using rating scales (Zenga, 1990). Many scales have international reach with the advantage of having databases available, being able to compare the performance of organizations, and identifying meaningful standards. It is not our intention to go into the merits of these tools, since the task of the corporatist is to understand their objectives and then use the results obtained. In cases where beneficiaries are able to make judgments about the performance received, satisfaction measures can be used as performance indicators because they represent a check on the pursuit of the productive mission.

5.7 Customer/user service perception

In nonprofit organizations, as we have already seen in Section 4.12, two aspects of the quality of goods and services provided can be identified:

- the quality referred to the objective and structural traits of the goods/services;
- the quality perceived by the recipients of the goods and services.

These two aspects are complementary to each other. The quality level of production depends not only on the degree of quality of individual components or infrastructure, but also on how well the goods and services are received by the beneficiaries and how well their expressed needs are met. In order to assess effectiveness, it is essential to analyze the "external" profile of the nonprofit organization, identified in the relationship that exists between the provision of the service and the users' perception of it. The goods and services that enable the achievement of institutional purposes must be neither excessive in relation to the needs of the beneficiaries, to avoid waste of resources, nor insufficient, to avoid a large percentage of subjects being dissatisfied. We can calculate the service utilization level (Arduini, 1996) by referring to the following concepts:

- volume of services provisioned, understood as the volume of resources produced by the company and made available to potential users;

- volume of services provided, thus indicating the level of services actually used by users;
- volume of services requested, as a quantification of the volume of demand from potential beneficiaries.

The indicators that can be analyzed are:

$$\text{service offer index} = \frac{\text{Services provided}}{\text{Services provisioned}}$$

$$\text{service demand index} = \frac{\text{Services provided}}{\text{Services requested}}$$

The intensity of service use depends on the combination of demand and supply. To obtain this information, the crowding index can be calculated:

$$\frac{\text{offer index}}{\text{demand index}} = \frac{\text{Services provided}}{\text{Services provisioned}} \times \frac{\text{Services requested}}{\text{Services provided}}$$

$$= \frac{\text{Services requested}}{\text{Services provisioned}}$$

For a correct interpretation, it should be noted that a surplus of the supply of services over demand shows that the volume of services produced is greater than the volume of services requested and thus delivered, in which case the crowding indicator will be less than unity. In the opposite case, where there is a situation of exuberance of demand over supply the crowding indicator will be greater than unity. Other indicators can be used that express the ability of nonprofits to attract recipients of the service offered. For example, the ratio of actual users to potential users can be calculated:

$$\frac{\text{actual users}}{\text{potential users}}\%$$

This indicator shows the interest the organization generates in its beneficiaries. To calculate and interpret it, however, it will be necessary to have information about the environment in which the organization operates and to consider the presence or absence of organizations offering similar services.

5.8 The degree of user satisfaction

In order to assess the degree of satisfaction of the recipients, it will be necessary to know the opinion of the users. Only in this way will it be possible to know how recipients perceive certain quality aspects of services. Normally, the degree of satisfaction is directly related to important elements of the service such as the characteristics and care of facilities, the timing of services, interpersonal relations between staff and users, and so on. Regarding staff relations, the degree of user satisfaction highlights the ability to understand the user's needs, to respect and understand individuals, to communicate and dialogue, to engage, and so on. Various methodologies can be followed to collect data on beneficiary consensus:

- carry out informal interviews;
- draw up questionnaires;
- compile statistics on the degree of abandonment or fidelity of beneficiaries.

The most commonly used method is questionnaires. In drafting them, it is necessary to divide the beneficiaries into groups according to characteristics deemed important, such as age or income level, and so on. Of course, this tool can be used only in the event that the respondents are able to answer the questions comprehensively. In the event that this method is not applicable, we employ statistical processing aimed at observing the changes experienced by a sample of beneficiaries representative of the user population. Once satisfaction has been measured, it can be complex to interpret the data collected because of the difficulty in making comparisons with other organizations. One problem often encountered is that of the diversity of scales used or surveyed people (Larsen et al., 1979). In these cases, the abandonment rate should be calculated, which indicates the percentage of users who give up using certain services with reference to a given period of time. Another indicator that can be calculated is the user turnover rate, which highlights the average time with which a given group of beneficiaries renews itself due to some leaving and others entering.

5.9 The promoting subject satisfaction indicators

The organization must meet the expectations of the promoting entity consisting of the core group that has set up and governs the organization. The fulfillment of the productive mission, which is identified in the improvement of the state of welfare of the beneficiaries, constitutes the main source of satisfaction of the individuals who form the promoting entity. They, having no economic interest, base their satisfaction on the ability of the organization to fulfill the productive function for which it was created. Normally, the motivations that drive promoters to engage in a nonprofit are related to a sense of usefulness, self-esteem, social recognition, and other motivations connected to the sphere of values and ideals. Achieving the goals enables these individuals to satisfy the needs and aspirations that are placed at the origin of their commitment. One indicator that can be used is aimed at highlighting the growth of the users' state of welfare:

$$\frac{\text{State of welfare year}(n) - \text{State of welfare year}(n-1)}{\text{State of welfare year}(n-1)}$$

Or it may be significant to detect the change in the number of users:

$$\frac{\text{users year}(n) - \text{users year}(n-1)}{\text{users year}(n-1)}$$

5.10 Employee satisfaction indicators

To achieve its goals, the nonprofit organization will need to value and satisfy both paid and volunteer employees. Employee satisfaction is of primary importance because it acts in two directions:

- it affects the quality of the activity;
- it affects the relationship mode with users and consequently the degree of satisfaction of service beneficiaries.

The following indicators could be used to analyze the satisfaction of volunteer employees:

$$\frac{\text{hours of voluntary work referred to a period}}{\text{volunteers}}$$

This indicator measures the number of hours each volunteer devotes on average to the organization. A significant amount of hours indicates a strong involvement of this category of employees with the organization; it also correlates with the quality of the contribution made. An indicator of the degree of loyalty of volunteer employees could be:

$$\frac{\text{volunteers working for over "n" years}}{\text{volunteers}}\%$$

As interaction skills with users mature over time, corporate seniority identifies not only the degree of employee satisfaction but also the quality of services provided. Another indicator that could be significant is volunteer turnover:

$$\frac{\text{Volunteers who left the company in the year}}{\text{volunteers}}\%$$

To analyze employee satisfaction, a number of indicators can be calculated that highlight employee satisfaction by linking it to turnover:

$$\frac{\text{employees working for over "n" years}}{\text{employees}}\%$$

This indicator, in addition to showing the degree of employee satisfaction, could also give important information about the accumulated experience in the organization. It is assumed that a higher accumulated experience corresponds to higher quality and quantity of work. Of course, in order to analyze this quotient it is necessary to know the reality of the organization because in cases where radical changes have been introduced the employees with the most seniority might be the least willing or least flexible to change. Another indicator that is possible to calculate is:

$$\frac{\text{employees who left the company in the year}}{\text{employees}}\%$$

This indicator should be analyzed in combination with the previous one and highlights both the degree of satisfaction and the quality of human resources. The degree of satisfaction can also be analyzed by checking the absenteeism rate:

$$\frac{\text{employee days of absence}}{\text{contract work days}}\%$$

An indicator can be calculated to show the degree of employee satisfaction related to flexible work management:

$$\frac{\text{part-time employees}}{\text{employees who have requested}}\%$$

The degree of employee satisfaction could also be examined by preparing questionnaires or by observing personnel management with regard to employee involvement in decision-making processes, the importance attached to ideas for business improvement identified by workers, the quality of teamwork, etc. In order to preserve and nurture the productive mission and employee loyalty, the pursuit of the productive mission itself is essential. Employees often conceive of work as a kind of mission. The strong identification with the productive mission that is created leads them to value the organization's effectiveness as a reason for gratification and as an element of support and reinforcement of work commitment. This is valid for employees, but is even more emphasized for volunteers who have no expectation of remuneration. The lasting commitment of volunteers is determined not only by the good working climate, but also by the possibility of personal development and the opportunity to bring benefits to users.

5.11 Other stakeholders' satisfaction indicators

In addition, the organization will have to meet the expectations of other stakeholders from whom it receives natural, human, and financial resources that assume a decisive role in its survival and development, with special emphasis on public and private entities that make contributions to the organization. Public entities will pay special attention to the achievement of the goal of improving the welfare status of users since rational allocation of resources will be related to the effectiveness of the action of the funded entity. The public entity should disburse funds after analyzing similar nonprofit organizations and selecting those that achieve the goals. Private individuals will be interested in knowing the results achieved to see concretely where their money has been used. Although some nonprofits are convinced that it is enough to talk about needs to receive donations, normally those who pour money in want to see results (Drucker, 2012). To analyze the degree of satisfaction of these stakeholders, the following ratio can be calculated:

$$\frac{\text{Donors giving funds for "n" years}}{\text{Donors}}$$

The quotient indicates the degree to which donors are loyal and thus the degree to which their expectations are met. The increase in the number of donors could be calculated as follows:

$$\frac{\text{New donors in the year}}{\text{Total donors at year-end}}$$

Where the quotient emphasizes the organization's ability to involve new people. In addition, the increase in average contributions could be calculated:

$$\frac{\text{Average contribution per donor year(n)} - \text{Average contribution per donor year(n} - 1)}{\text{Average contribution per donor year(n} - 1)}$$

The report indicates the organization's ability to increase the average annual contribution from supporters. Other indicators that can be used in the analysis of the degree of satisfaction of "other stakeholders" include those related to the measurement of corporate image by taking into account the company's fame and prestige, trust placed by corporate stakeholders, trust and consensus in local settings, and so on (Invernizzi & Molteni, 1992).

5.12 Communication and financial reporting as instruments of teleonomy

In private, non-state-funded, non-mutual nonprofit organizations, i.e., those for which the supporters of the organization are not also the exclusive beneficiaries of the activities carried out by the organization itself, communication is called upon to play a rather complex and articulated strategic role (Oliveira, Melo & Gonçalves, 2016; Wiggill, 2011). These nonprofits are simultaneously targeting two distinct markets:

- the supporters market, which they must preside over in order to gather the human and financial resources necessary for the development of their institutional activities;
- The organization's customers with whom they must deal, i.e., those who benefit from its activities.[3]

The communication activities of nonprofit companies are aimed at achieving two macro-objectives:

- attracting the resources needed to maintain the organization through fundraising mailings, seeking sponsorships from businesses, with campaigns to attract volunteers, etc.;
- achieve their mission (such as, for example, campaigns against smoking, forest fires, birth control, etc.).

These companies must operate in two distinct markets: that of customers and that of supporters. They must therefore adopt different strategies and tools that must complement and support each other. Sometimes the two sides of communication clash in terms of the type of message conveyed or the tools used. The overall coordination of communication activities is difficult both from a strategic and organizational point of view, but it is indispensable in order to effectively and efficiently achieve the mission. Traditional means of fundraising (Bennett, 2018; Kim, Gupta & Lee, 2021) include both direct and personal contact with the potential donor/funder as well as impersonal and/or indirect contact. The tools that involve personal contact with the potential donor are telemarketing and mailing, while the traditional impersonal means aimed at fundraising are events, promotions, advertising, public relations, or campaigns. In order to support these initiatives, aimed at a selected public, the role played by the mass media is fundamental, since they not only provide powerful support to these campaigns, but also play, if involved in a complete, open and articulate manner, the important role of guarantors for the public and donors. In fact, the media can be useful tools for denouncing social injustice and raising public awareness, as well as a way of making the nonprofit organization known to the general public. Above all, the third sector succeeds in activating territorial resources, creating an enlarged community bond that works as a kind of glue between the subjects of the community. A new area, useful for fundraising and means in general, somehow innovative, has arisen with the development of so-called ethical finance (Barbu & Boitan, 2019) which uses particular financial instruments (basically represented by ethical banks, ethical accounts, and ethical mutual funds) to support the nonprofit sector. All fundraising operations presuppose the external communication of one's own mission, one's own ideal; they are aimed at, or have as their objective, the consolidation of the nonprofit organization and its legitimization by the entire community: citizens, institutions, public bodies, etc. The activity of the nonprofit company is aimed at satisfying the needs and expectations of different stakeholders (Dempsey, 2018; Knox & Gruar, 2007), i.e., categories of stakeholders, which we could summarize in the following classes:

• both explicit and implicit customers/users, taking into account all those who can benefit from it;
• promoting entity constituted by the nucleus that set up and governs the company;
• collaborator, both paid and volunteer, i.e., all carriers of the work factor;
• other interlocutors from which the company receives natural, human, and financial resources that play a decisive role for survival and development, in particular public and private entities that make contributions to the company.

In nonprofit organizations there is a lack of proprietary interests that normally, in companies, are the first to pursue the management, stimulating its economy and efficiency. On the other hand, there are various and different concomitant interests in management and, consequently, transparency is necessary to guarantee information about the use of funds contributed by various donors in various capacities or of work done for free (Cabedo et al., 2018; Gazzola et al., 2021; Ortega-Rodríguez, Licerán-Gutiérrez & Moreno-Albarracín, 2020). Service users also have a special interest since there is often no free market, and therefore one cannot count on the efficiency for such services, that can normally be pursued through the mechanisms of free competition, which in any case do not apply here. The State has also provided specific tax benefits to these organizations for the special purposes of social activity that they carry out, supporting or sometimes replacing the State itself. A nonprofit organization will have as a condition of existence the satisfaction of the expectations of (Borzaga & Santuari, 2003):

• customers/users through the production of goods or the provision of services at levels deemed satisfactory, of adequate quality and at the cheapest possible price;
• promoting subjects, expectations that can be of different kinds: of esteem, self-realization, satisfaction of others' needs, etc., are linked to the fact that the nonprofit organization is born from the initiative of people motivated by philanthropic, religious,

cultural intentions, and who personally commit themselves with their work and with financial resources; the organization means through which to promote the diffusion of ethical values, the development of culture, science, or art, to provide assistance to people in need;

- collaborators, by offering adequate monetary remuneration, if they are paid, and fulfilling their aspirations to the best of their ability, both in the case of paid and voluntary collaborators; these organizations are based on a strong ethical motivation that allows them to benefit from the free, voluntary commitment of people who are willing to see their ideals fulfilled;

- other interlocutors from which the organization receives natural, human, and financial resources, particularly public and private entities that make contributions to the organization, the organization becomes the instrument for satisfying man's need to see certain ideals of life fulfilled, to contribute to the improvement of the society to which they belong, to help fellow human beings in difficulty.

Therefore, it becomes necessary to allow for closer scrutiny of the direct or indirect use of both public and private resources with or without restricted allocation. This function also fulfills the purpose of enabling future resourcing for its mission. This guarantee is fundamental both for relations with the State, which has the possibility of confirming or allocating funding or contributions according to what has been done, and also for relations with private individuals or other entities that can contribute with donations to the institutional aims. The financial statement is a summary document intended to represent the management of an economic entity over a period of time. It is the result of the representation of the management events and operations interpreted and reclassified through a properly structured accounting system (Adamo et al., 2018; Atrill & McLaney, 2008; Giunta & Pisani, 2005; Paolone & De Luca, 2004). For not-for-profit companies it is necessary to draw up financial statements in connection with the relationships they establish with the outside world, the risks that are taken, the financing or the donations granted, even if the purpose of such financial statements is different from that of businesses (Parsons & Trussel, 2008). Considering the Italian situation, the Code of the Third Sector establishes the minimum content of the financial statements that organizations are required to prepare. In particular:

- third sector entities with revenues, returns, proceeds, or income, however, denominated, not less than € 220,000.00 must prepare a financial statement for the year (accrual basis) consisting of

  - balance sheet;
  - management report;
  - mission report (document illustrating the budget items as well as the economic and financial performance of the institution and the way in which it pursues its statutory aims);

- entities with revenues, income, or receipts however denominated of less than € 220,000.00 may prepare a budget (cash principle) in the form of:

  - cash flow report.

This document, intended as a company financial statement, includes the main data on which the subjects outside the company can base their judgments and appreciations. However, the information on the life of nonprofit organizations should be made explicit in a document that is broader than the company financial statement and that gives an account, not only of the economic and financial situation, but also on the pursuit of the mutual and social purpose, on the results of the action carried out in relation to the local community, on the organizational and internal decision-making dynamics. Over time, other documents have spread in the nonprofit sector to accompany the annual report (Bartocci & Picciaia, 2015):

- the balanced scorecard (Kaplan & Norton (1992): is a strategic performance measurement tool that provides four perspectives for evaluating an organization's activities: financial, customer, internal business processes, learning and growth;
- social reports, environmental reports, and sustainability reports: developed at the same pace as the evolution of Corporate Social Responsibility and Sustainability, they represent documents in which the organization specifies the impacts of its activities on the community (the first), on the environment (the second), and on society, the environment and future generations (the third). These documents are consistent with the triple bottom line approach (Elkington & Rowlands, 1999);
- intangibles reports: documents reporting the organization's intangible capital (relational, human, intellectual).

It is possible to appreciate the organization's activity both from an internal point of view, regarding its efficiency for its stakeholders, and from an external point of view, regarding the benefits that management brings to the environment. In order to identify the functions of the organization's financial statements we look at the organization from an internal point of view. The balance sheet appears as the corporate document aimed at presenting the results of the organization's activities and can therefore be considered a model of management. If we were to change the point of observation and consider the activity from the outside, we could consider the information insufficient. The organization's balance sheet would provide us with information on the efficiency levels achieved by the organization (endogenous teleonomy), but it would not be sufficient to represent the overall impact of the activity on the macro-system (exogenous teleonomy). In order to allow an evaluation of the activity and its results from an external point of view, it is advisable to elaborate the sustainability report with the function of completing the information offered by the balance sheet with regard to the social implications of the organization's activity (exogenous teleonomy).

5.13 The sustainability report

If the corporate balance sheet allows to appreciate the efficiency of the organization (endogenous teleonomy), the effectiveness can be evaluated through the exogenous teleonomy indicators exposed in this chapter. Nonprofit organizations have an ethical obligation to their stakeholders and the public to conduct their activities with accountability and transparency. According to Meyer, Ferrari, and Zoebeli (2012) a comprehensive way to be transparent is to produce an annual report to accompany the financial statements. The organization can show in a document the mail results, services, and financial data with photos and graphs and make them readily available to the public by posting them on the website (Zainon et al., 2013). Since it is a voluntary document, there is currently no general and unique standard for its drafting; therefore, each organization can choose the format closest to its situation and size, choosing from the most popular national and international models (e.g., GRI, SASB, and the future IFRS sustainability disclosure standards, ESRS). The more accountable and transparent an organization is, the more it will be trusted by the public, donors, constituents, and regulators. Nonprofit organizations voluntarily disclose information about their ethical behavior and their relationships with the social and natural environment for the economic, image, and credibility benefits that arise, which increase the overall value of the organization. There are many reasons for a nonprofit organization to implement a sustainable reporting process (Gazzola, Ratti & Amelio, 2017):

- to improve reputation (BSR, 2011; Ernst & Young, Boston College Center for Corporate Citizenship, 2013);
- to improve economic, social, and environmental impacts on society and communicate these impacts to stakeholders;
- to create positive relationships with the corporate world;
- to improve efficiency;
- to attract top talent;
- to attract the best donors;
- to fulfil employee expectations;
- to dialogue and engage with stakeholders;
- to be transparent;
- to ensure internal governance, ethics, and risk management practices.

Drafting the annual report and the sustainability report could be considered contrary to the principle of unity of management operations. It would be like arguing that there is one budget intended for internal use and another intended for the social system. These criticisms are aimed at highlighting the need for an appropriate information tool that is not necessarily derived from accounting. In the nonprofit sector too, it would be possible to speak of an integrated report, meaning a document containing qualitative and quantitative information linked both to endogenous and exogenous teleonomy, thus allowing an overall measurement of the performance of nonprofit organizations, overcoming the current fragmentary nature of measurements. This implies the need to articulate a system of information that leads to propose a single qualitative-quantitative document, possibly to be standardized through the delimitation of the fields on which to report, the standardization of the vocabulary used, the classification of headings and the adoption of a unified nomenclature. This integrated report should combine the economic dimension (endogenous) and the social/environmental dimension (exogenous), making use of the system of indicators highlighted in this study. If there is relevant regulation and literature on integrated reporting for the second sector (Busco et al., 2013; De Villiers & Hsiao, 2017; Dumay et al., 2016; Soriya & Rastogi, 2021; Vaz, Fernandez-Feijoo & Ruiz, 2016; Vitolla, Raimo & Rubino, 2019), the same cannot be said for this particular model of nonprofit organization (Adams & Simnett, 2011; Dameri & Girella, 2019; Ferrando, 2019; Maroun & Lodhia,

2017; Pärl et al., 2020). A complete assessment of the performance of nonprofit organizations therefore requires the preparation of an integrated report, a document derived from the second sector but which also lends itself to be used within the third sector.

5.14 The integrated report for nonprofit organizations

Integrated reporting is defined by the IIRC (International Integrated Reporting Council) as "a concise communication about how an organization's strategy, governance, performance and prospects, in the context of its external environment, lead to the creation, preservation or erosion of value over the short, medium and long term" (IIRC, 2021). The integrated report was created with the ultimate aim of merging the different forms of communication of the organization (efficiency and effectiveness data) into a single document, in order to provide an exhaustive and total vision not only of the organization but also of its dimensions. It does not, however, represent a simple evolution of the documents that preceded it and their informative capacity, but is the tool for a new form of communication aimed at highlighting to external stakeholders relationships between the various economic, social, environmental, and strategic dimensions. Understood with a broader meaning than the canonically adopted one, the concept of "value" expressed by integrated reporting also includes other types of values such as environmental and social ones that the classical doctrine, focused on "economic value", usually does not consider (Guatri, 1998). The attention to the needs of each stakeholder allows to have an overall and clearer evaluation of the value created by an organization and considers the success of an organization as the ability to simultaneously create value for shareholders and society in general (Krzus, 2011). Moreover, the integrated report, considering value in a broader sense, considers intangible assets (human, relational, structural capital), which the annual report tends to exclude or limit (Giovanardi & Gambetti, 2012; Salvi et al., 2020). The use of the integrated report, however, does not only meet the stakeholders' need for information, but it is also a useful and important tool for the organization itself, as it allows to analyse the relationships between financial and nonfinancial performance and encourages the implementation of an internal integration process. It therefore becomes necessary for the organization that wants to approach this communication tool, the adoption of an integrated thinking (integrated thinking: "the active consideration by an organization of the relationships between its various operating and functional units and the capitals that the organization uses or affects. Integrated thinking leads to integrated decision-making and actions that consider the creation, preservation or erosion of value over the short, medium and long term"). In concrete terms, integrated thinking implies the creation of a corporate structure that allows the establishment of solid and lasting relationships between the subjects that make up the different business areas, and that also duly takes into account the environmental, social, strategic, and relational factors that affect it, thus obtaining a complete and integral view of the organization (Al-Htaybat & von Alberti-Alhtaybat, 2018; Bridges, Yeoman & Harrison, 2020). In recent years (in 2013 and then in 2021), in order to develop a framework on integrated reporting and to harmonize regulation at the international level, IIRC published the International <IR> Framework (Biondi, Dumay & Monciardini, 2020; Gerwanski, Kordsachia & Velte, 2019; Marrone & Oliva, 2019). It does not force the adoption of particular measurement methodologies or performance indicators; this framework provides the principles to allow individual companies to consider the specific characteristics of their own reality, while allowing a certain degree of compatibility among their reports (principle-based approach) (Tiron-Tudor, Oprisor & Zanellato, 2019).

The integrated report – with a view to making the value creation process explicit – must highlight (as process inputs) six categories of capital (not only tangible):

- financial capital: this is generated through the result of investments, operating activities or is raised through financings such as bonds, equity, or debt;
- manufactured capital: represents all buildings, machinery, plant, infrastructure, equipment, or other physical objects;
- intellectual capital: refers to those intangible assets pertaining to organizational capital as well as to the value attributed to knowledge itself;
- human capital: this capital is made up of all the resources provided by the people involved in the organization's activities, expressed in terms of skills, knowledge, abilities, and experience, as well as their motivation to be an active part of the organization;
- social and relationship capital: this is made up not only of the organization's ability to communicate information that increases the welfare of its stakeholders and the community in which it operates, but also of the relationships established with them;
- natural capital: represents the environmental resources, whether renewable or not, used by the organization to carry out its activities (e.g., air, forests, water).

The framework in its second section outlines the seven guiding principles to be used as a basis for the preparation and presentation of the report, and lists its content elements. The guiding principles are:

1   strategic focus and future orientation: this principle expresses the need for the integrated financial statements to include information on the strategy adopted, its impact on the ability to create value over a given period of time (short/medium/long-term) and the use of the various capitals, but at the same time advocates the inclusion of other data relating to aspects other than strategy. For example, the opinion of governance members on the ability to define strategic directions based on past experience;

2   connectivity of information: if the organization adopts an integrated way of thinking, this principle is easy to apply. This, in fact, allows to bring to light the relationship between all the factors that influence the creation of value for the organization, providing an overall view;

3   stakeholder relationships: this principle underlines the importance of reporting information concerning the relationships established with stakeholders and the organization's sensitivity to their information needs;

4   materiality: this principle encourages organizations to provide, within the integrated financial statements, only and exclusively the information inherent to the factors actually related to the creation of value, whether in the short, medium or long term;

5   conciseness: the financial statements must provide relevant and concise information, leaving out those that would weigh down and compromise its transparency and clarity;

6   reliability and completeness: information should be unbiased, clear, and free from material error. All material information should also be disclosed, regardless of whether it is negative or positive;

7   consistency and comparability: between one year and the next, the organization must use documents produced following the same methodologies and reporting policies, unless there are changes strictly necessary to increase the quality of the information reported.

The content elements are:

1   organizational overview and external environment: "What does the organization do and what are the circumstances under which it operates?"

2 governance: "How does the organization's governance structure support its ability to create value in the short, medium and long term?"

3 business model: "What is the organization's business model?"

4 risks and opportunities: "What are the specific risks and opportunities that affect the organization's ability to create value over the short, medium and long term, and how is the organization dealing with them?"

5 strategy and resource allocation: "Where does the organization want to go and how does it intend to get there?"

6 performance: "To what extent has the organization achieved its strategic objectives for the period and what are its outcomes in terms of effects on the capitals?"

7 outlook: "What challenges and uncertainties is the organization likely to encounter in pursuing its strategy, and what are the potential implications for its business model and future performance?"

8 basis of presentation: "How does the organization determine what matters to include in the integrated report and how are such matters quantified or evaluated?"

While this document is primarily aimed at for-profit companies, the principles guiding integrated reporting are also an appropriate framework for not-for-profit organizations (Adams & Simnett, 2011; Purcell, 2020).

The predominantly social vision of nonprofit organizations should also lead nonprofit organizations to adopt an integrated view in order to assess the overall performance of the entity, i.e., the two dimensions of endogenous and exogenous teleonomy. However, there are barriers (Adams & Simnett, 2011) in applying the IIRC framework to the third sector:

- the framework, as an international regulation, could encounter regulatory obstacles in the different countries where it is applied. This is true for the for-profit sector as well as for the nonprofit sector where the legislation of individual countries is even more fragmented and uneven than in the for-profit sector. This short-term issue can be overcome over a longer-term time frame;

- integrated measurement and reporting may be difficult to implement in small contexts or contexts where the organizational-managerial vision is less present;

- excessive disclosure of sensitive information could discourage the adoption of integrated reporting.

To overcome these challenges, nonprofits could provide for an interim phase, where existing reports are adapted to the framework, without initially being published. Economic analysis alone is not sufficient to assess the performance of such organizations, but it is necessary to combine it with the analysis of sustainability dimensions. Therefore, it would be appropriate to prepare an integrated report that combines the economic and financial dimensions with the pillars of sustainability, as in the case of companies in the second sector. In fact, nonprofit organizations can obtain significant advantages by overcoming a reporting based on the mere compliance with prescriptive standards, in favour of a more flexible reporting, focused on the organization and aiming at the externalization of other values. In Italy, as well as in other countries, nonprofit organizations operate in different sectors of activity and therefore have different objectives. In order to assess this diversity, it is appropriate to encourage them to adopt integrated and flexible reports, adaptable to the context rather than prescriptive. Nonprofit organizations, moreover, are already active in the management of a multiplicity of capitals, often intangible, which, as said, are not represented in the financial statements. Intangible capital is more important in nonprofits than in for-profits (think of the importance of reputation to obtain donations). Nonprofits are therefore already in line with the value creation process identified by the IIRC, however it does not apply to the communication of organizations or to reporting. What is relevant is that current measurement systems based on short-term input/output measures tend to underestimate nonfinancial and intangible outcomes and impacts. In a world where resources are becoming increasingly scarce, strategy, the founding element of integrated reporting, is also an element that nonprofit organizations already consider. In fact, they must try to act strategically to obtain funds and donations. The increasing complexity in accessing funding and the growing disclosure/reporting burden imposed by governments and funders also pushes nonprofits in this direction. Nonprofits must therefore improve their reporting and communication practices to make the process that leads to real value creation more transparent. They need to increase stakeholder engagement, making individuals and groups accountable to each other and allowing for increasing and equal interaction (Brown & Dillard, 2014). A recent publication (note: Pärl et al., 2020) highlighted the adoption of the IIRC framework by nonprofit organizations. The authors demonstrated that nonprofits spontaneously adopt some elements of the IIRC framework and can benefit from full implementation. In the literature, as mentioned above, academic contributions on integrated reporting in the nonprofit sector are still limited (Villiers, Rinaldi & Unerman, 2019); only some studies (Amagoh, 2015) focus on the applicability of IR to nongovernmental organizations.

Integrated reporting however (Dameri & Girella, 2019) needs adaptations in order to better consider the specificities of nonprofit organizations. The third sector presents assessment methodologies that differ from those provided for the second sector, mainly due to the presence of four elements: intangible assets, temporal and scale interdependencies, the need for collaboration between people with divergent viewpoints and path dependence (Castillo, 2018). The integrated report model is a solution of this as it combines the multiplicity of capitals from the past, influential in the present, and in the future, which contribute to the creation of value. The main issues arising from the application of the IIRC framework to the nonprofit sector are:

1   "The primary purpose of an integrated report is to explain to providers of financial capital how an organization creates, preserves or erodes value over time" (p. 5). It is evident that the main recipients of the integrated report are the providers of financial capital. While this makes sense in the for-profit sector, it is less relevant in the not-for-profit sector, where organizations are defined as "ownerless" and therefore the identification of providers of capital as key stakeholders would be irrelevant. The integrated report in the nonprofit sector should provide neutral information to all stakeholders, without distinction. The framework then continues "an integrated report benefits all stakeholders interested in an organization's ability to create value over time, including employees, customers, suppliers, business partners, local communities, legislators, regulators and policy-makers" (p. 5), being more coherent with the vision of the third sector;

2   the value creation scheme ("Process through which value is created, preserved or eroded") is more consistent with the second sector, where governance is more structured and the business model is more easily identifiable. In the nonprofit sector, the multiple input-output relationships are more complex, also by virtue of the different types of organizations and the considerable interests at stake.

To date, there is no reference framework for nonprofit organizations, despite the obvious limits of financial reporting in the evaluation of corporate performance (*single bottom line*). This limitation can be partially overcome by adapting the IIRC framework to the nonprofit sector, in order to prepare an integrated report that combines the dimensions of endogenous and exogenous teleonomy in a single document, thus achieving a better appreciation of the overall performance of the nonprofit organization.

Notes

1 By the term "issue" we mean any perception of a difference between desired goals and actual degree of goal achievement.
2 To identify the state of welfare, the concept of outcome is used.
3 In for-profit companies, on the other hand, the figure of the supporter and that of the customer coincide, given that the customer pays a price for the products he/she receives.

References

Abzug, R., & Webb, N. J. (1999). Relationships between nonprofit and for-profit organizations: A stakeholder perspective. *Nonprofit and Voluntary Sector Quarterly, 28*(4), 416–431.

Adamo, S., Lionzo, A., Incollingo, A., & Fellegara, A. M. (2018). La "nuova" informativa di bilancio: Profili teorici e criticità applicative dopo il D. Lgs. 139/2015 e i nuovi principi OIC. Milano: Franco Angeli, 1–410.

Adams, S., & Simnett, R. (2011). Integrated reporting: An opportunity for Australia's not-for-profit sector. *Australian Accounting Review, 21*(3), 292–301.

Ahmed Alarussi, A. S. (2021). Effectiveness, efficiency and executive directors' compensation among listed companies in Malaysia. *SAGE Open, 11*(4), 21582440211054129

Al-Htaybat, K., & von Alberti-Alhtaybat, L. (2018). Integrated thinking leading to integrated reporting: Case study insights from a global player. *Accounting, Auditing & Accountability Journal. 31*(5), 1435–1460.

Amagoh, F. (2015). Improving the credibility and effectiveness of non-governmental organizations. *Progress in Development Studies, 15*(3), 221–239.

Arduini, S. (1996). *Le aziende nonprofit: Il controllo dell'efficacia e dell'efficienza*. Torino: Giappichelli.

Atrill, P., & McLaney, E. J. (2008). *Financial accounting for decision makers*. Pearson Education.

Barbu, T. C., & Boitan, I. A. (2019). Ethical financing in Europe-non-parametric assessment of efficiency. *Sustainability, 11*(21), 5922.

Bartocci, L., & Picciaia, F. (2015). *Accountability e organizzazioni non profit. Quale possibile ruolo per il reporting integrato?. Colloquio scientifico sull'impresa sociale, IX edizione*. Università degli Studi Mediterranea di Reggio Calabria.

Bennett, R. (2018). *Nonprofit marketing and fundraising: A research overview*. Routledge.

Biondi, L., Dumay, J., & Monciardini, D. (2020). Using the international integrated reporting framework to comply with EU directive 2014/95/EU: Can we afford another reporting façade?. *Meditari Accountancy Research, 28*(5), 889–914.

Borgonovi, E. (1995). *Aziende non profit: problemi teorici, profili giuridici e politiche di indirizzo.* Clueb.

Borzaga, C., & Santuari, A. (2003). New trends in the non-profit sector in Europe: The emergence of social entrepreneurship. In OECD (2003), *The non-profit sector in a changing economy, local economic and employment development (LEED).* Paris: OECD Publishing, 31–59.

Bridges, C. M., Yeoman, M., & Harrison, J. (2020). Integrated thinking or integrated reporting, which comes first?. In C. De Villiers, P. C. K. Hsiao, & W. Maroun (Eds.). *The Routledge handbook of integrated reporting* (pp. 241–250.) Routledge.

Brown, J., & Dillard, J. (2014). Integrated reporting: On the need for broadening out and opening up. *Accounting, Auditing and Accountability Journal, 27*(7), 1120–1156.

BSR (2011). State of Sustainable Business. GlobeScan, 2011 Poll, BSR.

Busco, C., Frigo, M. L., Riccaboni, A., & Quattrone, P. (2013). *Integrated reporting. Concepts and cases that redefine corporate accountability.* Springer Cham.

Cabedo, J. D., Fuertes-Fuertes, I., Maset-LLaudes, A., & Tirado-Beltrán, J. M. (2018). Improving and measuring transparency in NGOs: A disclosure index for activities and projects. *Nonprofit Management and Leadership, 28*(3), 329–348.

Castillo, E. A. (2018, October). Qualities before quantities: A framework to develop dynamic assessment of the nonprofit sector. In *Nonprofit policy forum (Vol. 9*, No. 3). De Gruyter.

Crawford, L., Morgan, G. G., & Cordery, C. J. (2018). Accountability and not-for-profit organisations: Implications for developing international financial reporting standards. *Financial Accountability & Management, 34*(2), 181–205.

Dameri, P., & Girella, L. (2019). Putting integrated reporting where it was not: The case of the not-for-profit sector. *Financial Reporting, 2*, 111–140.

Dempsey, A. L. (2018). Adding the stakeholder value: Governance convergence in the private, public and not-for-profit sectors. In I. Demirag (Ed.). *Corporate social responsibility, accountability and governance* (pp. 147–164). Routledge.

De Villiers, C., & Hsiao, P. C. K. (2017). Integrated reporting. In C. De Villiers, P. C. K. Hsiao, & W. Maroun (Eds.). *Sustainability accounting and integrated reporting* (pp. 13–24). Routledge.

Drucker, P. F. (1963). *Managing for business effectiveness.* Harvard Business Review.

Drucker, P. F. (1994). *Managing the non-profit organization-practices and principles.* London: Butterworth.

Drucker, P. (2012). *Managing in a time of great change.* Routledge.

Dumay, J., Bernardi, C., Guthrie, J., & Demartini, P. (2016, September). Integrated reporting: A structured literature review. In *Accounting forum (Vol. 40*, No. 3, pp. 166–185). Elsevier.

Elkington, J., & Rowlands, I. H. (1999). Cannibals with forks: The triple bottom line of 21st century business. *Alternatives Journal, 25*(4), 42.

Ernst & Young, Boston College Center for Corporate Citizenship (2013). *The value of sustainability reporting*. Ernst & Young, Boston College Center for Corporate Citizenship.

Ferrando, P. M. (2019). Integrated reporting e creazione di valore tra profit e non profit. Il caso dell'Associazione Gigi Ghirotti. *Impresa Progetto, 2*, 1–19.

Gazzola, P., Amelio, S., Papagiannis, F., & Michaelides, Z. (2021). Sustainability reporting practices and their social impact to NGO funding in Italy. *Critical Perspectives on Accounting, 79*, 102085.

Gazzola, P., Ratti, M., & Amelio, S. (2017). CSR and sustainability reporting for nonprofit organizations. An Italian best practice. *Management Dynamics in the Knowledge Economy, 5*(3), 355–376.

Gerwanski, J., Kordsachia, O., & Velte, P. (2019). Determinants of materiality disclosure quality in integrated reporting: Empirical evidence from an international setting. *Business Strategy and the Environment, 28*(5), 750–770.

Giovanardi, M., & Gambetti, R. C. (2012). *Integrated annual reporting and corporate performance: an intangible-based communication perspective. Managing corporate communication: A cross-cultural Approach*, London: Palgrave Macmillan, 373–393.

Giunta, F., & Pisani, M. (2005). *Il bilancio*. Apogeo Editore.

Guatri, L. (1998). *Trattato sulla valutazione delle aziende*. Milano: Egea.

Handy, F., & Brudney, J. L. (2007). When to use volunteer labor resources? An organizational analysis for nonprofit management. *Departmental Papers (SPP), 91*.

IIRC (2021). INTERNATIONAL <IR> FRAMEWORK.

Invernizzi, G., & Molteni, M. (1992). *Analisi di bilancio strategica. Strumenti per valutare posizione competitiva, vulnerabilità, patrimonio intangibile.* Milano: Etas Libri SpA.

Kanter, R. M., Stein, B. A. (1979). *Growing pains in life in organizations: Workplaces as people experience them*. New York: Basic Book.

Kaplan, R. S., & Norton, D. P. (1992). The balance scorecard – measures that drive performance. *Harvard Business Review, 70*(1), 71–79.

Kasim, T., Haracic, M., & Haracic, M. (2018). The improvement of business efficiency through business process management. *Economic Review: Journal of Economics and Business, 16*(1), 31–43.

Kim, S., Gupta, S., & Lee, C. (2021). Managing members, donors, and member-donors for effective nonprofit fundraising. *Journal of Marketing, 85*(3), 220–239.

Knox, S., & Gruar, C. (2007). The application of stakeholder theory to relationship marketing strategy development in a non-profit organization. *Journal of Business Ethics, 75*(2), 115–135.

Krashinsky, M. (1997). Stakeholder theories of the non-profit sector: One cut at the economic literature. *Voluntas: International Journal of Voluntary and Nonprofit Organizations, 8*(2), 149–161.

Krzus, M. (2011). Integrated reporting: If not now, when?. *Fuer International Rechnungsleggung, 6*, 271–276.

Larsen, D. L., Attkisson, C. C., Hargreaves, W. A., & Nguyen, T. D. (1979). Assessment of client/patient satisfaction: Development of a general scale. *Evaluation and Program Planning, 2*(3), 197–207.

Maroun, W., & Lodhia, S. (2017). Sustainability and integrated reporting by the public sector and not-for-profit organizations. In C. De Villiers, & W. Maroun (Eds.). *Sustainability accounting and integrated reporting* (pp. 101–120). Routledge.

Marrone, A., & Oliva, L. (2019). Measuring the level of integrated reporting alignment with the< IR> framework. *International Journal of Business and Management, 14*(12), 110–120.

Meyer, B., Ferrari, D., & Zoebeli, D. (2012). Transparency of NPOs' financial reporting: A quantitative study of annual reports (Switzerland). ISTR-Conference in Siena, July.

Mouzas, S. (2006). Efficiency versus effectiveness in business networks. *Journal of Business Research, 59*(10–11), 1124–1132.

Minahan, S., & Inglis, L. (2005). Stakeholders and strategic planning in non-profit organisations: Case studies in complexity and conflict. *Third Sector Review, 11*(2), 17–33.

Oliveira, E., Melo, A. D., & Gonçalves, G. (Eds.). (2016). *Strategic communication for non-profit organizations: Challenges and alternative approaches.* Vernon Press.

Ortega-Rodríguez, C., Licerán-Gutiérrez, A., & Moreno-Albarracín, A. L. (2020). Transparency as a key element in accountability in non-profit organizations: A systematic literature review. *Sustainability, 12*(14), 5834.

Paolone, G., & De Luca, F. (2004). *Il bilancio di esercizio. Funzione informativa, principi, criteri di valutazione.* Torino: Giappichelli.

Pärl, Ü., Paemurru, E., Paemurru, K., & Kivisoo, H. (2020). Dialogical turn of accounting and accountability integrated reporting in non-profit and public-sector organizations. *Journal of Public Budgeting, Accounting & Financial Management, 34*(1), 27–51.

Parsons, L. M., & Trussel, J. M. (2008). Fundamental analysis of not-for-profit financial statements: An examination of financial vulnerability measures. *Research in Government and Nonprofit Accounting, 12*, 65–75.

Purcell, J. (2020). A case study on (and case for) integrated reporting and integrated thinking: Relevance to a not-for-profit professional accounting association. In *The Routledge handbook of integrated reporting* (pp. 93–104). Routledge.

Salvi, A., Vitolla, F., Raimo, N., Rubino, M., & Petruzzella, F. (2020). Does intellectual capital disclosure affect the cost of equity capital? An empirical analysis in the integrated reporting context. *Journal of Intellectual Capital, 21*(6), 985–1007.

Soriya, S., & Rastogi, P. (2021). A systematic literature review on integrated reporting from 2011 to 2020. *Journal of Financial Reporting and Accounting, 20*(3/4), 558–579.

Tiron-Tudor, A., Oprisor, T., & Zanellato, G. (2019). The mimicry of integrated reporting: An analysis of the principles-based approach. *Integrated reporting* (pp. 153–168). Cham: Springer.

Usai, G. (1990). *L'efficienza nelle organizzazioni*. Torino: Utet.

Vaz, N., Fernandez-Feijoo, B., & Ruiz, S. (2016). Integrated reporting: An international overview. *Business Ethics: A European Review, 25*(4), 577–591.

Villiers, Ch., Rinaldi, L., & Unerman, J. (2019). Integrated reporting: Insights, gaps and an agenda for future research. *Accounting, Auditing and Accountability Journal, 27*(7), 1042–1067.

Vitolla, F., Raimo, N., & Rubino, M. (2019). Appreciations, criticisms, determinants, and effects of integrated reporting: A systematic literature review. *Corporate Social Responsibility and Environmental Management, 26*(2), 518–528.

Wiggill, M. N. (2011). Strategic communication management in the non-profit sector: A simplified model. *Journal of Public Affairs, 11*(4), 226–235

Zainon, S., Hashim, M., Yahaya, N., & Atan R. (2013). Annual reports of Nonprofit Organizations (NPOs): An analysis. *Journal of Modern Accounting and Auditing, 9*(2), 183–192.

Zenga, M. (1990). *Introduzione alla statistica descrittiva*. Milano: Vita e pensiero.

6 Conclusions: The Use of the Indicator System

6.1 The conditions of exogenous teleonomy

The use of performance measure indicators makes it possible to interpret the dynamics of business phenomena relevant to the achievement of objectives (Franceschini et al., 2019; Mella, 2012; Star et al., 2016). The measure system is also intended to guide and stimulate behaviors consistent with the goals to be achieved. In order to interpret the phenomena of nonprofit organizations, it is necessary to remember that for nonprofit organizations the fulfillment of institutional purposes is the condition of existence that allows the organization to have a lasting life. Such organizations are able to survive in the environment in which they carry out their institutional activities if they are able to satisfy the goals while maintaining the conditions of exogenous teleonomy. In fact, the ensogenic teleonomy of the nonprofit organization is determined by the environment's ability to sustain systems that the environment considers useful. For this reason, the result of their actions should not be evaluated in relation to the increase in wealth, measured by the contrast of exchange values (price-revenue and price-cost), or by the size of the wealth distributable among those who have contributed to production, but rather in relation to the quantity and quality of the needs satisfied, i.e., the "utility" produced. (Borgonovi, 1995). The evaluation of the organizaton's performance must be carried out taking into consideration its productive mission, by bearing in mind the lasting growth of the organization and, above all, the satisfaction of all key stakeholders. In nonprofit organizations, the achievement of institutional objectives requires not only the realization of economic balance and an adequate level of efficiency, but also the achievement of managerial effectiveness. For an assessment of the achievement of management objectives, special attention needs to be paid to indicators that are designed to show the

DOI: 10.4324/9781003350439-7

degree of user satisfaction. Measures of user satisfaction assume relevance both internally and externally. Information regarding the satisfaction of the structure, employees, and processes can help identify strengths and weaknesses and plan any changes to be made. The degree of user satisfaction also makes it possible to determine the organization's image and is a determining factor in the degree of satisfaction of the promoting entity, donors, and employees. The achievement of goals allows the promoting parties to satisfy the needs and aspirations that are placed at the origin of their commitment, related to the sense of usefulness, self-esteem, social recognition, and other motivations linked to the realm of values and ideals. For employees, who view labor as a sort of mission, the effectiveness of the organization is a reason for gratification and is an element that supports and reinforces work commitment. Especially for volunteers, who have no salary expectations, lasting commitment is related not only to the positive work climate but also to the possibility of personal development and the opportunity to bring benefits to users. Donors, both public and private, also pay special attention to the achievement of the goal of improving the welfare status of users as they will want to know the results achieved in order to tangibly verify where the donated money has been spent. The appreciation and acceptance of the community will enable the nonprofit organization to elicit and guarantee the inflow of contributions, donations, and the availability of human resources and professions over time. Nonprofit organizations have the potential to be seen as trying to elicit acts of liberality from volunteers, who provide labor, and from donors, and turn these acts into useful "things" that can meet needs, and increase the welfare status of beneficiaries (Capaldo, 1996).

6.2 Improving performance: Maximizing efficiency

Performance measurement must be able to encourage behaviors aimed at improving services. Therefore, the nonprofit organization, after analyzing the extent of achievement of institutional goals, will have to verify that it has operated efficiently with respect to endogenous teleonomy, i.e., the system's ability to maintain its structure. This verification can be carried out by analyzing performance indicators and other efficiency indicators.

It is not enough to measure performance; it is necessary to improve it through a process that allows for the identification and removal of weaknesses and increased levels of efficiency and effectiveness. To maintain and improve these results, while respecting the achievement of objectives, the nonprofit organization may apply the criterion of maximum efficiency (Ezzamel, 1996), also called the criterion of minimum means for maximum results.

This criterion can be applied:

- when different alternatives are possible, depending on the information available;
- when it is possible to express all particular choice criteria in terms of comparable outcomes and measurable sacrifices.

When there are several alternatives available for achieving the goal, preference should be given to:

- the alternative that, given equal results, requires the least sacrifice, if the possible alternatives differ in sacrifices;
- the alternative that, given equal sacrifice, allows for maximum achievement, if the possible alternatives differ in results;
- the alternative for which the ratio of achievable results to necessary sacrifices is greatest, if with the possible alternatives different results are obtained with different sacrifices, a ratio that can be calculated as follows:

$$\text{efficiency} = \frac{\text{achievable benefits}}{\text{necessary sacrifices}}$$

The choice of the most cost-effective business operations should be determined by taking into account that:

- most business operations require a sacrifice, and that sacrifice is often measurable in terms of the value of resources expended in implementing those operations;
- on the other hand, the benefits and results of implementing most business operations are sometimes quantifiable in terms of "results" or costs avoided, or if that is not possible they can be expressed in quantitative terms.

In this case it is possible to compare the sacrifices, on the one hand, considering them as costs, and the benefits on the other.

6.3 The cost-effectiveness (affordability) objective

The fact that these organizations do not have economic purposes, but rather social and humanitarian ones, does not affect their operations;

the cost-effectiveness of a company is independent of the nature of its institutional purpose. If we analyze efficiency in terms of sacrifices and benefits, this criterion can also be expressed as a decision criterion of maximal cost-effectiveness. When there are alternative management operations to achieve given goals, the decisive criterion of maximal cost-effectiveness is expressed in these terms:

- prefer the alternative with which the lowest costs are associated for the same outcome;
- prefer the alternative that yields the greatest outcome or cost savings, for the same cost;
- prefer the alternative that allows for a higher cost-effectiveness ratio (generalized):

$$E = \frac{\text{results (cost saving)}}{\text{cost}}$$

When decisions concern economic units, production processes, or entire economic coordinations of nonprofit organizations, the criterion of maximal cost-effectiveness is not sufficient because it does not take into account that in order to bear the costs, and to achieve the corresponding results, the use of financial resources, i.e., capital investment, is required.

Therefore, it is necessary to observe not only the cost-effectiveness of different coordinations, but also the amount of capital required to carry out the different alternatives. In choosing between different alternatives characterized by the same cost-effectiveness, which require, in addition, different amounts of capital:

- prefer the alternative that has the highest cost-effectiveness for the same amount of capital required;
- prefer the alternative that requires the least amount of capital for the same cost-effectiveness.

In order to decide rationally, it is necessary to consider the different alternatives and specify for each one the degree of cost-effectiveness in terms of economic efficiency and financial efficiency, taking into account the previously indicated ratios. Maintaining a self-sustaining economic and financial balance represents the condition of lasting functionality; a prolonged imbalance would lead to the termination of the activity. The assessment of economic viability in nonprofit organizations should not be carried out only by taking into account the break-even in accounting terms, but should be interpreted as the growth and enhancement of the asset of resources and the maintenance over time of the conditions to meet and guarantee the expectations of stakeholders. The organization must implement a financial feeding mechanism of qualitative development because business functionality can only be maintained if continuous improvement in its performance is sought.

In conclusion, from the business model investigated it follows that the system of performance measures is expected to enable the monitoring of both the productive transformation, with the physical-technical efficiency indicators, and the economic transformation, with the economic efficiency indicators, the financial transformation with the financial efficiency indicators, and finally the managerial transformation with the effectiveness indicators, taking into account the degree of satisfaction of the expectations of the main categories of stakeholders. For the latter, as well as for second-sector organizations, the issue of social reporting (Costa & Goulart da Silva, 2019; Nardo & Siboni, 2018) and in particular the drafting and presentation of a sustainability report for third-sector companies is important (Gazzola et al., 2021). Economic analysis alone is not sufficient to assess the performance of such organizations, but it is necessary to combine it with the analysis of sustainability dimensions (Ortega-Rodríguez, Licerán-Gutiérrez & Moreno-Albarracín, 2020). It therefore becomes advisable to prepare an integrated report in the third sector as well, a report that combines economic and financial dimensions with the pillars of sustainability (Ferrando, 2019; Pärl et al., 2020) in order to reach a better overall assessment of organizational performance.

References

Borgonovi, E. (1995). *Aziende non profit: Problemi teorici, profili giuridici e politiche di indirizzo*. AAVV, Clueb.

Capaldo, P. (1996). *Le aziende non profit: definizioni e classificazioni. Aa. Vv., Le aziende non profit tra stato e mercato*. Bologna: Atti del convegno Aidea, Clueb.

Costa, E., & Goulart da Silva, G. (2019). Nonprofit accountability: The viewpoint of the primary stakeholders. *Financial Accountability & Management*, 35(1), 37–54.

Ezzamel, M. (1996). *La misurazione e la valutazione della performance divisionale: Parametri contabili, finanziari e qualitativi*. Milano: EGEA.

Ferrando, P. M. (2019). Integrated reporting e creazione di valore tra profit e non profit. *Il caso dell'Associazione Gigi Ghirotti. Impresa Progetto*, 2, 1–19.

Franceschini, F., Galetto, M., Maisano, D., & Neely, A. D. (2019). *Designing performance measurement systems. Theory and practice of key performance indicators*. Cham: Springer Management for professionals.

Gazzola, P., Amelio, S., Papagiannis, F., & Michaelides, Z. (2021). Sustainability reporting practices and their social impact to NGO funding in Italy. *Critical Perspectives on Accounting, 79*, 102085.

Mella, P. (2012). Performance indicators in business value-creating organizations. *Economia Aziendale Online, 2*(2), 25–52.

Nardo, M. T., & Siboni, B. (2018). Requirements and practices of social reporting in Italian not-for-profit organisations. In R. Tench, B. Jones, & W. Sun (Eds.). *The critical state of corporate social responsibility in Europe (Critical studies on corporate responsibility, governance and sustainability, Vol. 12).* Bingley: Emerald Publishing Limited, 299-317.

Ortega-Rodríguez, C., Licerán-Gutiérrez, A., & Moreno-Albarracín, A. L. (2020). Transparency as a key element in accountability in non-profit organizations: A systematic literature review. *Sustainability, 12*(14), 5834.

Pärl, Ü., Paemurru, E., Paemurru, K., & Kivisoo, H. (2020). Dialogical turn of accounting and accountability integrated reporting in non-profit and public-sector organisations. *Journal of Public Budgeting, Accounting & Financial Management, 34*(1), 27–51.

Star, S., Russ-Eft, D., Braverman, M. T., & Levine, R. (2016). Performance measurement and performance indicators: A literature review and a proposed model for practical adoption. *Human Resource Development Review, 15*(2), 151–181.

Index

Printed in the United States
by Baker & Taylor Publisher Services